LEGENDS OF TEAM CANADA

Joe Pelletier

Warwick Publishing

Introduction: Canada's Team

WHICH SPORTS TEAM CAN JUSTIFIABLY CALL ITSELF "CANADA'S TEAM"?

Obviously, that title would have to belong to a hockey team. With all due respect to professional and amateur football, baseball, basketball, soccer, and lacrosse teams in this country, as well as Olympic team sports such as figure skating and curling, no sport has been and will continue to be as universally and rabidly followed in Canada as hockey.

The Montreal Canadiens and Toronto Maple Leafs might each have a claim on the title. Both of these National Hockey League franchises have been around for nearly a century and have had legendary players and teams that formed long-standing dynasties. The two clubs have engaged in a struggle with each other for hockey superiority seemingly since the beginning of time. They have had epic battles spanning several generations, and for the longest time were the only two choices Canadians had to cheer for. Montreal was generally the team of Quebec and the Atlantic, Toronto the team of Ontario and the west. Although it was not hard to find supporters in enemy territory, try as they might, neither team could ever quite properly attain the title of Canada's Team.

More recent NHL entries from Vancouver, Edmonton, Winnipeg, Quebec, Calgary, and Ottawa have all attempted to stickhandle away the title, some more successfully than others. Only the Edmonton Oilers, fuelled by Wayne Gretzky and the last great NHL dynasty, came close to achieving the status of Canada's Team.

Only one hockey team can truly lay claim to the title of Canada's Team. The only Canadian team to have the unconditional support of all Canadians — whether they are from French Canada or English Canada, whether they are young or old, whether they are hockey fans or not — is Team Canada.

While many NHL teams garner interest far beyond municipal and even provincial boundaries thanks to their longevity and glorious history, none enjoys the nationwide fan support of Team Canada.

Unlike those professional teams, Team Canada is a collection of great hockey players who come together for only a brief period of time to represent our nation at hockey's most prestigious international tournaments. We cheer them on for a period of days, not years, as they chase after international hockey supremacy, not the Stanley Cup, only to see them disperse just as quickly and rarely get back together again.

Hockey's heads of state — Mark Messier, Wayne Gretzky, and Mario Lemieux — gather to celebrate a goal in Game Two of the final round series against the Soviet Union during the 1987 Canada Cup at Hamilton's Copps Coliseum.

Clockwise from top left. This page: Phil Esposito, the emotional catalyst for Canada's victorious squad in the 1972 Summit Series, delivers a sporting salute at the Luzhniki Arena in Moscow; Wayne Gretzky hoists the Canada Cup trophy aloft as Team Canada celebrate their dramatic three-game triumph over the Soviet Union in the 1987 Canada Cup; goaltender Bill Ranford proudly waves the Canadian flag as he celebrates Canada's 1994 triumph at the World Championships, its first since 1961; Bobby Orr enjoys a laugh while posing for photographers in the jersey of his #4 counterpart from Czechoslovakia after the final of the 1976 Canada Cup.

Clockwise from top left. Opposite page: Mark Messier and Edmonton Oiler team-mate Glenn Anderson share a happy moment after the 1987 Canada Cup victory; Team Canada bench rises to join a goal celebration (from left, Rod Gilbert, Serge Savard, Bill White, Peter Mahovlich, Dennis Hull and Jean Ratelle); Team Canada gathers for the now-traditional casual team portrait after winning the 1987 Canada Cup; Martin Lapointe raises his arms in triumph as teammates surround him in celebration after Canada's dramatic 3-2 victory over the Soviet Union in the final game of the 1991 World Junior Championships in Saskatoon.

Team Canada takes many forms. In any given season, Team Canada is the brand name given to the men and women chosen to represent our nation at regular tourneys such as the world championships, the world junior championships, and the Olympics. Sometimes professional hockey's best get together in top-level tournaments that we all embrace, even though it often happens at unusual times, such as late summer.

They did not do it for money or prestige, but for love — the love of Canada, and the love of Canada's game.

To become a Team Canada legend is no easy task. To make the team is nearly impossible. Only twenty to twenty-five players can comprise the final roster, even though the talent pool is often much deeper. It is often said that Canada is the only nation that could legitimately ice two or even three teams that would all have a serious chance of capturing victory.

Obviously the players who do make the cut are already the best of the best. But to become a legend, the player must still do something extraordinary while wearing the red and white uniform. That could come in the form of repeated strong performances over the course of a career. It could mean an outstanding single tournament performance that will never be forgotten. Or it could mean scoring the big goal that immortalizes that player forever.

In *Legends of Team Canada,* we honour the men and the women who have taken this country to hockey superiority. They did not do it for money or prestige, but for love — the love of Canada, and the love of Canada's game. The best of the very best are all here.

We start with a look at the heroes of the 1972 Summit Series team. That team was the first to be dubbed Team Canada, and its members established the standards that all future Canadian stars would have to live up to. The gutsy and inspiring play of blue-collar hockey stars such as Phil Esposito, Bobby Clarke, and Paul Henderson displayed what it meant to be a Canadian hockey player. For all the hockey skills that are observable by statistics, it is the immeasurable intangibles that separated Canadians from the rest of the hockey world. They wore the maple leaf on their heart, never considered defeat and, in typically dramatic fashion, pulled out a thrilling victory. From that memorable high point we move on to the Canada Cup tournaments, later renamed the World Cup of Hockey. The tournament has now spanned three decades, and has seen new heroes arise each time. Darryl Sittler, John Tonelli, Mark Messier, Wayne Gretzky, and Mario Lemieux are among the legends that carried on the Canadian hockey tradition, allowing hockey fans across the globe to witness the greatest hockey ever played.

Canada's favourite annual international hockey tournament, the World Junior Hockey Championships, is not overlooked. For some of these junior heroes the Championships are their first steps towards NHL stardom, while for others these games represent the peak of their otherwise unnoticed careers. Here we pay tribute to both types.

Though Canadian hockey fans have historically dismissed the world championships as unofficial, we remember the key contributors and key moments from both the amateur and modern eras. We also pay homage to earlier versions of Team Canada. This includes pre-1960 Canadian amateur teams who represented Canada at the Olympics and the world championships. We also look at the two defunct versions of the Canadian national team. In these cases many of the players could not make it as NHL competitors, yet would become legends of Canadian hockey nonetheless.

And of course we look at the modern Olympics. Coming off the heels of double gold medal victories in the 2002 Salt Lake City games, Canada's thirst for top-level international hockey is now quenched, for the first time, at the Olympic level. We honour the stars of both men's and women's versions of Team Canada.

From Paul Henderson to Mario Lemieux, from Wayne Gretzky to Hayley Wickenheiser, today's stars meet yesterday's heroes in these pages. Together they comprise the best that have ever represented our nation. These are the true Legends of Team Canada.

Key to Player Statistics

GP – Games Played	**Goaltender Stats:**
G – Goals	**W** – Wins
A – Assists	**L** – Losses
Pts – Points	**T** – Ties
PIM – Penalties In Minutes	**GAA** – Goals Against Average

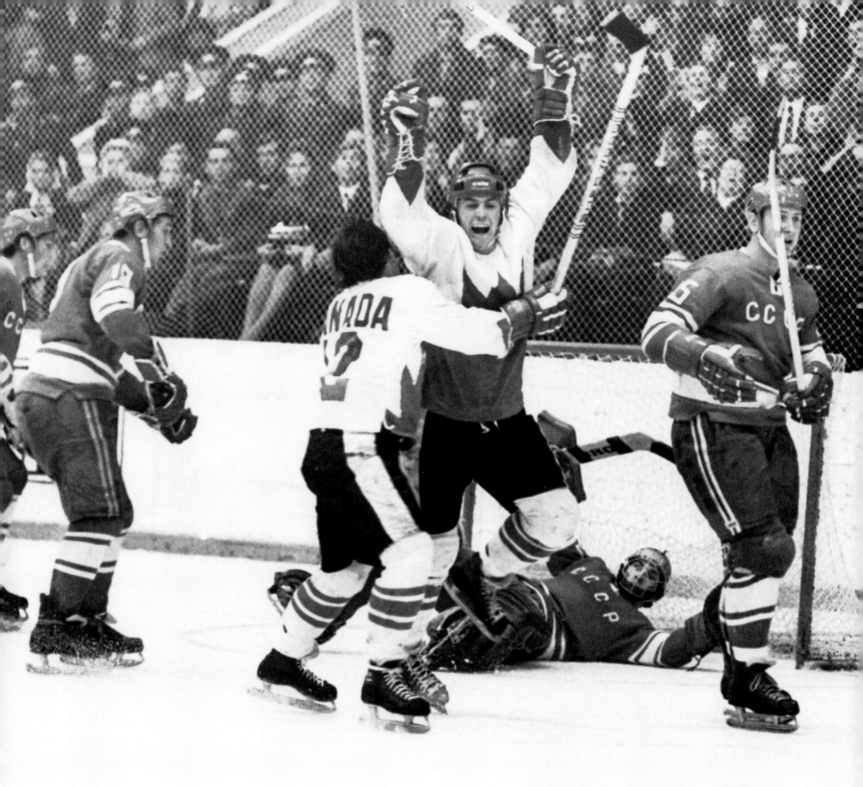

Above: Paul Henderson turns away from a beaten Vladislav Tretiak and into Yvan Cournoyer's embrace after scoring with 34 seconds left in the game to give Canada victory in the 1972 Summit Series.

Right: Nothing brings out Canadian pride like hockey, as this flag-waving group in Saskatoon demonstrate during the 1991 world juniors.

Left: Wayne Gretzky and teammates ignite their fans as they gather to celebrate a goal against Sweden during the 1991 Canada Cup in Toronto.

Paul Henderson

With 34 seconds left in the game, Paul Henderson slips the puck past Soviet goalie Vladislav Tretiak, scoring the winning goal that capped Canada's dramatic comeback victory in the 1972 Summit Series

ONE OF THE MOST MEMORABLE, INDEED LEGENDARY, HOCKEY photographs is that of Paul Henderson jumping into Yvan Cournoyer's arms after scoring the dramatic 1972 Summit Series winning goal with just thirty-four seconds left in the final game.

Yet unlike most legends of Team Canada, Henderson was not a particularly great player. He was a hard-skating and industrious winger with the Toronto Maple Leafs who happened to have a breakout season with thirty-eight goals in the 1970–71 campaign. Had he had a more typical season offensively, he might never have been invited to the inaugural Team Canada training camp.

But he was, and it was as if it were his destiny. Henderson would go on to have the greatest eight games of his life and become the ultimate Canadian hockey hero — the small-town, hard-working kid who scores the big goal.

Henderson was actually one of the last players to make the team. He had a terrific training camp along with linemates Bobby Clarke and Ron Ellis. All three were on the bubble as to whether or not they would make the team, but they played extremely well together. They were Canada's best threesome, and the only line that would be kept together throughout the series.

Paul Henderson — *Kincardine, Ontario*

Tournament	GP	G	A	Pts	PIM
1972 Summit Series	8	7	3	10	4
1974 Summit Series	7	2	1	3	0
Team Canada Totals	15	9	4	13	4

Henderson in particular was red hot throughout the entire series. He tied Phil Esposito and Alexander Yakushev for the series' goal-scoring lead with seven. He was especially hot in Moscow — he scored twice in Game Five and scored the game winners in Game Six and Game Seven, as well as the famous Game Eight.

The Game Seven goal was especially spectacular. With less than three minutes left to play, Henderson was sprung loose thanks to a nice pass from Serge Savard. Henderson was in alone on two Soviet defencemen, which was normally an impossible scoring chance. Henderson crossed so that the two defencemen were forced to swap their positions. During that confusion Henderson slipped the puck through defenceman Evgeny Tsygankov's legs and went around him. Instead of playing the man, Tsygankov tried to play the puck. He failed to stop the puck and Henderson was in alone. He lifted the puck just under the cross bar while falling down as the defenders tackled him.

But it was the dramatic series-winning goal in Game Eight for which Henderson will forever be remembered. Mid-shift, Henderson famously called Peter Mahovlich, another Summit Series standout, to the bench and jumped on. He raced into the Soviet zone and attempted to take an Yvan Cournoyer pass but was tripped up and crashed into the boards behind the net. He scrambled to his feet in time to gobble up a Phil Esposito rebound and take a shot on the Soviet goal. Again netminder Vladislav Tretiak stopped it, but a second rebound came to Henderson. This time he found a hole in Tretiak's seemingly impenetrable armour.

Henderson led Team Canada and 3,000 Canadian fans in Moscow in an outburst of celebration that was being matched by millions of Canadians back home. Some fans of that generation insist on calling it the greatest moment in Canadian history, not just Canadian hockey history.

At that instant, Henderson became a hockey immortal. He had not had a career anywhere comparable to a Rocket Richard, Gordie Howe, Bobby Orr, Wayne Gretzky, or Mario Lemieux, but by scoring this goal, he became every bit as legendary.

Though he will always be remembered for scoring "the goal heard around the world," it is often forgotten that Henderson also represented Team Canada in the World Hockey Association's copycat Summit Series of 1974, although for Henderson and the WHA, the result was drastically different (as can be seen in his Series stats above).

After leaving the National Hockey League, Henderson fizzled out from the hockey scene. He grew to regret scoring the famous goal, for it changed his life forever. Everyone expected him to be the hero on a nightly basis. He could not live up to the lofty expectations.

Finding refuge in religion, Henderson has rebounded to find inner peace and now embraces his hockey hero role. As time goes by, his legendary status only seems to increase. Now travelling Canada and the world as an inspirational speaker, it must be a rare day that goes by when he does not have tell the story of "the goal" one more time.

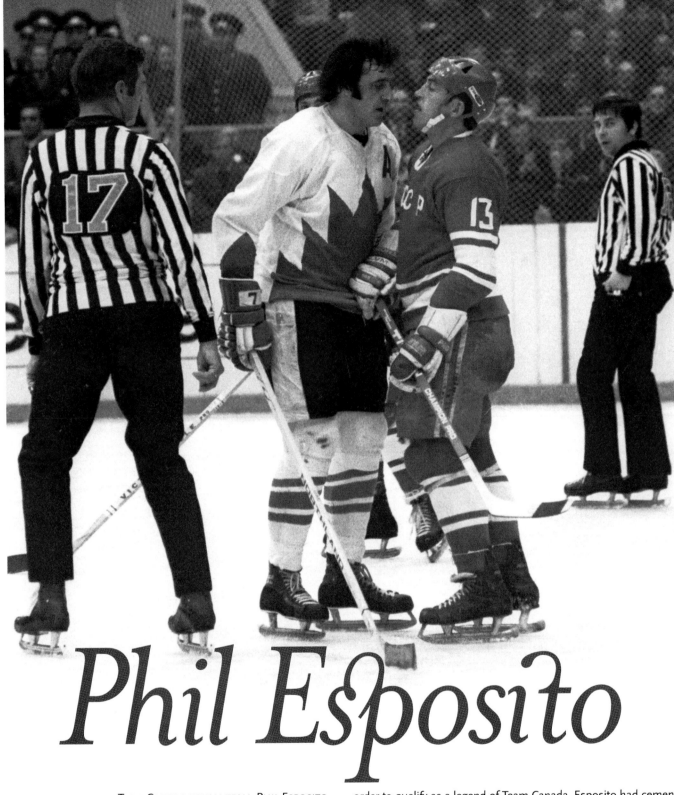

Phil Esposito

IF THERE WERE AN ALL-TIME TEAM CANADA DREAM TEAM, PHIL ESPOSITO would be the obvious choice as captain.

Esposito represented Canada three times. In 1976 he was a veteran influence on the powerhouse Canada Cup squad. He contributed four goals and seven points in seven games despite no longer being the offensive superstar he was earlier in the decade. In 1977 he rejoined Team Canada in the World Championships. He was the team's best player and scored seven goals and ten points in ten games. Unfortunately Canada did not earn a medal.

But Esposito never needed those two Team Canada appearances in order to qualify as a legend of Team Canada. Esposito had cemented his reputation as one of Team Canada's all-time greats in just eight games in a September to remember back in 1972.

While Paul Henderson has been forever immortalized for his series-winning heroics, Phil Esposito's effort in the tournament was equally memorable. In fact, almost every member of Team Canada would be quick to name Espo as the real hero of the series.

Right from the get-go, Esposito was the undisputed leader of this team. He had a commanding stature and he oozed charisma. Players were quick to literally follow him in training camp, at practices and

PHIL ESPOSITO — *Sault Ste. Marie, Ontario*

Tournament	GP	G	A	Pts	PIM
1972 Summit Series	8	7	6	13	15
1976 Canada Cup	7	4	3	7	0
1977 World Championships	10	7	3	10	14
Team Canada Totals	25	18	12	30	29

Opposite page: As game officials watch carefully, Phil Esposito confronts dangerous Soviet forward Boris Mikhailov.

This page: Espo at work in his office, pestering Soviet goalie Tretiak from the edge of his goal crease.

away from the rink. When his team struggled out of the gate, he fired them up and would not accept losing as an option. In fact, he never once felt Canada would lose, not even after falling behind 3-1-1 after five games against the impressive Russians.

No one was more intense than Espo. In the ceremonial puck drop before Game One, he vigorously attacked the puck on the usually friendly draw. Then just thirty seconds into the game he scored the series' opening goal and celebrated emphatically.

The Soviets soon proved they would be no pushover, and in fact dominated the rest of Game One, winning easily in Canada's cathedral of hockey — the Montreal Forum.

The humiliating defeat in Game One seemed easy to take compared to the Game Four loss. In the final game played in Canada, dejected Vancouver fans loudly booed Team Canada off the ice. That would be Team Canada's lingering reminder of their lack of success as they headed to the U.S.S.R. down 2-1-1.

But Espo would have none of that. He went on national TV after the game and, with his heart and the maple leaf on his sleeve, spoke his mind.

"To the people across Canada, we tried. We gave it our best. To the people who booed us, geez, all of us guys are really disheartened. We're disillusioned and disappointed. We cannot believe the bad press we've got, the booing we've got in our own building.

"I'm completely disappointed. I cannot believe it. Every one of us guys — thirty-five guys — we came out because we love our country. Not for any other reason. We came because we love Canada," he ranted off the top of his head and from deep in his heart.

Team Canada rallied after perhaps the most famous speech in Canadian history (yes, perhaps even more famous than any political speech ever offered). They headed to the U.S.S.R., and Soviet fans were quickly introduced to the Esposito charm. During the player introductions Phil slipped on a stem of one of the roses that had been handed out to the players moments earlier. The big Italian fell flat on his butt. The arena erupted in laughter that turned into cheers as Espo got up and blew a kiss into the crowd and took a bow.

From that very first introduction through every passionate moment he played in their country, Esposito endeared himself to Soviet hockey fans to the point that he remains a hockey legend there, too.

Canada unthinkably blew a three-goal lead in that first game in Moscow. That forced them to win all the remaining games. Thanks to Esposito's inspirational play and Henderson's timely goal scoring, Canada was able to save face and win the tournament.

Espo led the tournament in points and tied for the lead in goals scored. He was as charismatic as the Soviets were stone-faced, which was symbolic of the sharp differences between the two teams. He played the tournament as if possessed. He scored thirty seconds into the first game, and assisted on Paul Henderson's monumental goal with just thirty-four seconds left in Game Eight. Twice he was named the MVP of a game, and was instrumental in the Game Eight victory, scoring two goals and assisting on two others.

Paul Henderson has said that seemingly every day of his life someone thanks him for scoring the dramatic goal in Moscow. Thank you too, Phil Esposito.

Bobby Clarke

Bobby Clarke's relentless skating and forechecking kept Soviet defenders like Alexander Gusev(2) and Viktor Kuzkin(4) on their toes as they guarded goalie Vladislav Tretiak.

A TWENTY-TWO-YEAR-OLD BOBBY CLARKE LAUNCHED HIS CAREER INTO the superstar stratosphere in eight games in September of 1972. That may have come as a surprise to some, as he was the last player to make the Summit Series team.

The Philadelphia Flyers' infamous yet inspirational leader made a 1972 team loaded with centre icemen thanks largely to a great chemistry with scrimmage linemates Paul Henderson and Ron Ellis. Right from early on in the series this surprising trio emerged as Canada's most consistent line. Clarke is quick to credit the trio's status as borderline players as their biggest advantage in making the team, as they took the training and preparations more seriously than many of the superstars who were all but guaranteed a spot on Team Canada. Clarke earned the respect of many in the series for his determined play, his near-flawless faceoff ability, and his solid two-way play.

Though he played with heart and admiration, the "Flin Flon Bomber" also earned the hostility of many for a vicious two-handed slash on

Soviet superstar Valeri Kharlamov's hurt ankle in Game Six. Many fans, both in the U.S.S.R. and in later years in Canada, have chastised Clarke for this blatantly dirty play. It has become a trademark image for Clarke, who was known as a gritty but sometimes underhanded player who would do whatever it took for his team to win.

Clarke never apologized for the slash, which he refers to as a "tap on his sore ankle." Even years after the event Clarke refused to make excuses, saying it was a part of hockey, or at least a part of that heated series.

Over time, the slash has overshadowed his awesome play in the series. Clarke, who was third in Team Canada scoring with two goals and six points, was Canada's best player along with Henderson and Phil Esposito. He earned great praise from his teammates and the media alike for the maturation of his game and for his determined effort.

And that was not forgotten four years later when Clarke was named Canada's team captain in the inaugural Canada Cup Tournament. That team featured sixteen Hall of Famers and is often considered the best

Team Canada of them all. For Clarke to be named captain of that squad was quite the honour. Clarke, who had also captained the Flyers to two Stanley Cup championships in the previous couple of years, led the team to a 6-1 record, including classic showdowns with the Soviet Union and Czechoslovakia, en route to capturing what Canadians viewed as the first real world hockey championship, because NHLers were finally allowed to compete against the world's best.

Clarke would take only one further tour of duty with Team Canada as a player. In 1982 he came off a tough NHL season to join Team Canada in the World Championships, in which the team earned a bronze medal.

Following his retirement as a player Clarke put his vast hockey experience to good use and turned to managing hockey teams, most notably his beloved Philadelphia Flyers. He also had the opportunity to be a part of two Team Canada entries in the management category — as co-general manager in the unforgettable 1987 Canada Cup and as general manager of the 1998 Olympic team.

Clarke remains as controversial a figure as ever. Love him or hate him, you can't deny his contributions to Canada's success in the international arena. He continues to be a legend of Team Canada.

BOBBY CLARKE — *Flin Flon, Manitoba*

Tournament	GP	G	A	Pts	PIM
1972 Summit Series	8	2	4	6	18
1976 Canada Cup	6	1	2	3	0
1982 World Championships	9	0	1	1	6
Team Canada Totals	23	3	7	10	24

Serge Savard

SERGE SAVARD IS WITHOUT QUESTION ONE OF THE MOST SUCCESSFUL DEFENCEMEN IN TEAM CANADA HISTORY.

Aside from being one of the top defenders in hockey history and his standout play in two of the earliest international showdowns involving National Hockey League players, Savard's inclusion is necessary because of his excellent record against Canada's eternal rivals — the U.S.S.R. Between the 1972 Summit Series and the 1976 Canada Cup, Savard participated in a total of six contests against the Soviets while in a Team Canada jersey. By no coincidence, Team Canada's record with Savard in the lineup is an amazing 5-0-1.

Savard did not dress in the shocking opening-game loss in the Summit Series but was inserted into Games Two and Three, which resulted in a win and tie respectively. In that third game, however, Savard suffered a hairline fracture in his leg that he initially feared would cost him the rest of the series. Thankfully there was a ten-day break between Games Four and Five that allowed Savard to recuperate. He missed Game Four in Vancouver and Game Five in Moscow, both Canadian losses, but returned for the rest of the series. Canada would not lose another game and would come from behind to capture the championship, thanks in large part to the steady defence of the savvy Savard. Final score: Savard 4 — Soviets 0, with one tie.

Savard would put his undefeated streak on the line again four years later when he was one of sixteen Hall of Famers to don the Canadian jersey for the inaugural Canada Cup. Team Canada '76, picked as the best team of all time by Savard and many others, only met the Soviets once in this tournament. It was a convincing 3-1 Canadian victory that placed Canada in the championship finals against Czechoslovakia. Canada would go on to capture the first Canada Cup.

Further underlining Serge Savard's excellence while in the red and white jersey of Team Canada was his inclusion as first unit defenceman on The Sports Network's all-time Team Canada. In a 2002 collector's edition magazine special, the network named Savard and the incomparable Bobby Orr as Canada's top defensive tandem. This Canada Cup pairing was nicknamed The Rock (Savard) and The Roll (Orr). Other defencemen included on the team were Denis Potvin, Ray Bourque, Paul Coffey, Scott Niedermayer, and Gary Bergman.

Savard, a very successful businessman and hockey executive upon retirement, returned to Team Canada as an executive for the 1987 Canada Cup. Tournament and Team Canada co-ordinator Alan Eagleson put together an interesting collection of National Hockey League general managers to select and mould a Team Canada that would have to face perhaps their most daunting task — the Soviet KLM Line in their prime. Shutting down Vladimir Krutov, Igor Larionov, and Sergei Makarov, along with defensive partners Alexei Kasatonov and Viacheslav Fetisov, was of extreme importance, but there was much debate about how to accomplish it.

Savard, along with former teammates Phil Esposito (then general manager of the New York Rangers) and Bobby Clarke (general manager of the Philadelphia Flyers), favoured physical, defensive, "Canadian" hockey. Glen Sather and John Muckler, of the high-flying Edmonton Oilers, favoured fire-wagon hockey.

Eagleson forced all of these strong personalities to work together to create the best Team Canada available. The resulting team was arguably the most exciting and most resourceful Canadian team ever iced, as fans witnessed the greatest hockey ever played.

While much of the credit has gone to coach Mike Keenan and scoring stars Wayne Gretzky and Mario Lemieux, Serge Savard also deserves to be recognized for his contributions. He was vital in the creation of the intellectual coaching staff, which included his own NHL coach, Jean Perron. He was also influential in the naming of a few of the surprise inclusions on that team — specifically Normand Rochefort and Kevin Dineen.

On the ice and in the manager's seat, the work ethic and example set by Serge Savard have been of great benefit to Team Canada.

Serge Savard — *Montreal, Quebec*

Tournament	GP	G	A	Pts	PIM
1972 Summit Series	5	0	2	2	0
1976 Canada Cup	7	0	3	3	0
Team Canada Totals	12	0	5	5	0

Serge Savard's all-round abilities made him a key contributor to Team Canada. A superb defender in his own end, he could also lug the puck himself and spring forwards loose with precise passes.

Peter Mahovlich

PETER MAHOVLICH — *Timmins, Ontario*

Tournament	GP	G	A	Pts	PIM
1972 Summit Series	7	1	1	2	4
1976 Canada Cup	7	1	4	5	0
Team Canada Totals	14	2	5	7	4

Above: Peter Mahovlich eludes the checking efforts of Soviet forward Vladimir Vikulov.

Right: Mahovlich hangs out Vladislav Tretiak's laundry as he scores a vital, short-handed goal in Game Two of the 1972 Summit Series.

At first, big Pete Mahovlich may seem like a bit of a debatable addition to Team Canada's legends. But his role in two key Canadian championships has been largely overlooked. He achieved defining moments in a Team Canada uniform that give him the edge over other candidates.

The lanky pivot, along with his Hall of Fame brother Frank, was named to the inaugural Team Canada for the 1972 Summit Series. After Phil Esposito, Paul Henderson, and Bobby Clarke, Mahovlich was arguably the best forward for Canada in the tournament. He was a prime penalty killer and great team player. He has never gotten enough credit for his role in the series.

A few moments stick out when remembering Mahovlich in the series. The first is his spectacular goal in Game Two. While everyone remembers Paul Henderson's famous goal because of the dramatics, many remember Mahovlich's breakaway goal because of the artistry.

While killing a penalty, Mahovlich picked up a cleared puck near the centre line, skated in on the lone defender, Yevgeny Paladiev, and faked a heavy slapshot. When the defender froze as if to block the puck, Mahovlich deftly deked Paladiev and drove in alone on goaltender Vladislav Tretiak. "The Little M" faked a forehand shot, went to his backhand, and while falling on top of Tretiak managed to slip the puck into the net using his impressively long reach.

Another memorable moment occurred in Game Eight. At one point Canadian director Alan Eagleson became involved in a fracas with Soviet military men. The soldiers were about to haul Eagleson out of the rink when Team Canada, led by Pete Mahovlich, showed up and rescued Eagleson. The incident underlines that for Team Canada the tournament was much like a war. Here were hockey players battling the Soviet military to help out one of their own. It also signifies just how much of a leader Mahovlich was for this team, although given future events involving Eagleson, Mahovlich would jokingly wish he had never intervened.

The other famous moment involving Mahovlich was a line change. Mahovlich was out with regular linemates Phil Esposito and Yvan Cournoyer late in the third period of the tied Game Eight. Though his unit had not completed their shift on the ice, Mahovlich heard Paul Henderson yelling at him to come off. Mahovlich selflessly did. Henderson went out and subsequently scored the most famous goal in hockey history.

Mahovlich would also represent Team Canada in the 1976 Canada Cup, scoring one goal and four assists in seven games in that tournament. Often playing on an effective line and power play unit with Montreal Canadiens teammates Guy Lafleur and Steve Shutt, Mahovlich was the only Canadian skater to play in all seven contests and not make it into the Hockey Hall of Fame. Mahovlich is best remembered for an impromptu jersey-swapping ceremony with the Czechoslovakians at the conclusion of the tournament.

Unlike most hockey players, Mahovlich's contributions were not necessarily measurable by goals and assists. Often it is the intangibles that define the best of the best. Mahovlich displayed great selflessness. He had an infectious smile and a carefree personality. Whenever Team Canada got into tense moments in either of these great tournaments, the guys could always count on the jovial Mahovlich to lighten the mood. But when the game was entering key moments, Pete Mahovlich could always be counted on. He set a great example for the legends that followed.

Yvan Cournoyer

YVAN COURNOYER — *Drummondville, Quebec*

Tournament	GP	G	A	Pts	PIM
1972 Summit Series	8	3	2	5	2
Team Canada Totals	8	3	2	5	2

NICKNAMED "THE ROADRUNNER," YVAN COURNOYER WAS ONE OF THE FASTEST SKATERS OF ANY ERA, so it was no surprise that he was one of the players selected for the 1972 Summit Series. If there was one single Canadian player who could keep up with or even out-skate the swift Soviets, it was Cournoyer.

Of course, Cournoyer was much more than just speed on skates. He was a complete player — as good a playmaker as he was a goal scorer, and a good defensive forward. There was no doubt that he was one of the best players in the world in the early 1970s, and he showed it in the Summit Series.

However, Cournoyer's contributions to the inaugural Team Canada are often overshadowed by those of Paul Henderson and Phil Esposito. Cournoyer formed a magical connection with Esposito on Canada's top offensive line in the tournament. Esposito was the dominant skater in the series, but much of the credit must be given to Cournoyer, who created many of the opportunities.

Cournoyer's blazing speed was a constant threat to the Soviet defence throughout the series. The Russians could never shut down Cournoyer completely, so they were forced just to try to slow him down. In Game Two of the series, he blew past a Soviet defenceman to score an exciting and psychologically important, not to mention game-winning, goal. Years later the still-smiling Cournoyer said that the defenceman probably still had a cold from Cournoyer breezing by him so quickly. He scored key goals in Games Six and Eight as well.

Cournoyer was also instrumental in setting up the series-winning goal. It was he who intercepted a Soviet clearing attempt and fired a cross-ice pass to a streaking Henderson. Henderson was tripped up initially and unable to handle the puck. But the unit's big centreman, Esposito, was able to swat the puck beyond the lone Soviet defender and to Henderson directly in front of the net. Henderson of course was able to bang the puck behind the fallen Vladislav Tretiak. Henderson joyously jumped into Cournoyer's arms in hockey's most famous photograph.

The 1972 Summit Series was the only opportunity Cournoyer had to play for Team Canada. Yet it was something he will never forget. Cournoyer, a ten-time Stanley Cup champion with the Montreal Canadiens, was once asked if winning the Summit Series compared to a Stanley Cup. The answer was that the two were not even close, as the victory in 1972 was "ten times better."

One of the most famous questions Canadians of that generation can be asked is, "Where were you when Henderson scored against the Russians in 1972?" Yvan Cournoyer has the best answer of anybody:

"Where was I when Henderson scored? I was in Moscow and a moment later, he was in my arms."

Left: Yvan Cournoyer (left) and Phil Esposito combine to trouble the Soviet defence in Moscow in 1972.

Below, right: Cournoyer scores on Tretiak during Game Two of the Summit Series in Toronto.

Bobby Orr

Bobby Orr's bad knees robbed him of his best years and left him on the sidelines for long periods of time. That this phenom could not stay healthy is probably the greatest source of disappointment in hockey history.

Orr was without a doubt the shining star in the hockey world in 1972. Due to off-season knee surgery he was unable to play for Canada in the Summit Series. He was named to the team but never recovered sufficiently to play. Many believe that the eight-game series would have been decided long before the final game if Orr had been able to get out on the ice.

Yet Orr did practice lightly and travel with the team, and just having him around scared the Soviets, who were well aware of his capacity. Make no mistake about it, Orr was the ultimate warrior and he played through some horrific pain during much of his career, but he knew that there was no way he could play in 1972.

In 1976, hockey fans all over the world finally got the chance to see Bobby Orr play for Canada in the inaugural Canada Cup. It was the first time he had donned a Canadian sweater since his junior days. Orr has always maintained that playing in this tournament ranks right up there with his Stanley Cup wins in 1970 and 1972.

Orr was only in slightly better shape than he had been at the time of the 1972 series. He was playing virtually on one leg and constantly had to use packs of ice to cool down his swelling knee. Between games he had fluid removed from his knee and was in constant pain. It was not until then that many of his teammates, who of course were normally enemies on other NHL clubs, realized what a warrior Orr really was.

Orr never complained, although it was clear that he was seriously hurting. He was brilliant as he helped Canada capture the Canada Cup, sharing the point-scoring lead in the tournament and being selected as the tournament's Most Valuable Player.

He was particularly dominant in the round robin victory over the Soviet Union. Orr had no points in that game but controlled the play as only he could. On a team loaded with sixteen eventual members of the Hockey Hall of Fame, Orr was the best.

While no one will doubt his status as a hockey legend, the inclusion of Orr in the list of legends of Team Canada was initially debatable. Though he had the ability to have rewritten the 1972 Summit Series had he been completely healthy, we can only judge him based on seven games in September of 1976. He didn't have the longevity, and it could be argued he did not have a defining moment in a Team Canada uniform.

But after acquiring old video footage of the 1976 Canada Cup, and watching a hobbled Orr dominate the game against the Soviets in particular, there is no question that he had a defining game. And it was that game that the whole nation watched with an anticipation not seen before or since, as finally the great Orr would represent Canada against the Soviets. Orr came through brilliantly, and that is why he is included as a legend of Team Canada.

TSN agrees. They named Orr and Serge Savard as the first defence pairing on the "All Time Team Canada Dream Team" in a 2002 magazine special.

BOBBY ORR — *Parry Sound, Ontario*

Tournament	GP	G	A	Pts	PIM
1972 Summit Series	0	0	0	0	0
1976 Canada Cup	7	2	7	9	9
Team Canada Totals	7	2	7	9	9

Opposite page: Bobby Orr's amazing skating skills and strength allowed him to elude opponents seemingly at will. Knee troubles deprived him of more appearances for Canada.

Bobby Hull

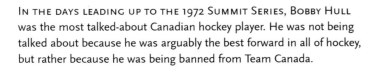

IN THE DAYS LEADING UP TO THE 1972 SUMMIT SERIES, BOBBY HULL was the most talked-about Canadian hockey player. He was not being talked about because he was arguably the best forward in all of hockey, but rather because he was being banned from Team Canada.

A few weeks prior to the selection of Team Canada 1972, Hull shocked the hockey world when he left the National Hockey League to accept a ghastly million-dollar contract from the Winnipeg Jets of the new major league rival World Hockey Association. By doing so he made himself ineligible for inclusion in the Summit Series, as it was agreed that Team Canada would be made up strictly of players under NHL contracts. Other WHA jumpers who likely would have made Team Canada '72 include Derek Sanderson, Gerry Cheevers, and J.C. Tremblay.

Hull's absence was a source of extreme controversy. Canadians from coast to coast complained loudly about his banishment, claiming that

Team Canada was misnamed, as it was really Team NHL. Even Canadian political leaders, who were in the midst of an election campaign, weighed in with their support for Hull's inclusion. It was the hottest topic of the summer.

With the loss of Hull and the injury to Bobby Orr, Team Canada was without its two most dynamic players. Had the duo played, perhaps the 1972 Summit Series would not have been such a close affair.

Hull did get the opportunity to play against the Soviets two years later, when the World Hockey Association held a copycat tournament known as the 1974 Summit Series. The Canadian side, made up entirely of WHA players, including a forty-six-year-old Gordie Howe and recent convert Paul Henderson, was not nearly as successful in 1974 as they were in 1972. The team only won once in eight games against a nearly identical Soviet squad.

BOBBY HULL — *Pointe Anne, Ontario*

Tournament	GP	G	A	Pts	PIM
1974 Summit Series	8	7	2	9	0
1976 Canada Cup	7	5	3	8	2
Team Canada Totals	15	12	5	17	2

Above: The Golden Jet, Bobby Hull, in full flight as he rounds the Czechoslovakian net. Left: Hull and Bobby Orr show off jerseys exchanged with their Czechoslovakian counterparts in 1976.

Fuelled by the desire to show up the NHL for its snub two years earlier, Hull was determined to be the difference-maker for Canada this time around. Playing on a line with Andre Lacroix and John McKenzie, he led all skaters with seven goals and nine points, including hat tricks in Games One and Four. Like Phil Esposito two years earlier, Hull became an instant folk hero in Russia for his incredible hockey ability. To this day Russian hockey fans still talk about the great "Booby" Hull.

The NHL would not ban Hull and other WHA converts in the only other top-level international tourney during the WHA's brief existence. In 1976, the Canada Cup was formed. Top players from the six major hockey nations were to compete in an all-but-official world championship. Canada included Hull, despite his continued carrying of the WHA crusade.

Hull was a dominant force in the inaugural Canada Cup, though Team Canada was extraordinarily deep. With sixteen players who would end up in the Hockey Hall of Fame, it was tough to spread out all the ice time. Many experts consider this team to be the greatest Team Canada of them all. But Hull stood out among all forwards, scoring a team-high five goals and finishing second in team scoring with eight points. Three of his goals were game-winning goals.

Bobby Hull ranks as one of the top ten greatest players in hockey history. But that alone does not assure a spot among the legends of Team Canada — just ask Patrick Roy. The furor over Hull's exclusion in 1972 may have helped him achieve legendary status in international hockey circles. When he finally had the chance to wear the Canadian jersey, all eyes were on him and he did not disappoint. That is why he ranks as a legend of Team Canada.

WHILE PAUL HENDERSON WILL ALWAYS HOLD THE TITLE OF ULTIMATE GOAL-scoring hero among Canadian hockey players, Darryl Sittler joined the short honour roll in 1976.

Sittler, the immensely popular Toronto Maple Leaf superstar, was named to Team Canada 1976 along with linemate Lanny McDonald. Together with Montreal defensive ace Bob Gainey, they formed a highly effective checking line that also chipped in with some timely offence.

Canada breezed through the round robin and opening game of the finals, but ran into turbulence in Game Two of the best of three final against Czechoslovakia. The Czechs, backed by a lanky goaltender named Vladimir Dzurilla, had control of the game late in regulation before Bill Barber scored to force overtime.

In overtime Canada took the play to the Czechs, but were continually stymied by Dzurilla. Fortunately for Canada, they had an observant assistant coach who told Sittler what he should try on his next scoring chance.

In a tale retold many times over the years on *Hockey Night in Canada*'s "Coach's Corner," Don Cherry advised his troops that the way to beat Dzurilla was to make him move in order to lose his angles. Cherry wanted Canadian shooters to hesitate on their shot just enough to step around the big but not overly agile netminder.

Darryl Sittler was obviously paying attention. Sittler took a quick Marcel Dionne pass in full stride and flew by the usually reliable Jiri Bubla into the Czech zone. Sittler then faked a small slapshot, forcing Dzurilla to commit to the shot that he thought was coming. Sittler pulled up on the shot and took a couple of extra strides to the outside before depositing the puck into a gapingly wide-open net at 11:36 of overtime.

For Sittler it was his fourth goal of the tournament, though no one remembers the other three. He, like Paul Henderson before him, is forever immortalized as a Team Canada hockey legend because of this famous goal.

Like Henderson, Sittler would, initially at least, receive many thank-yous from Canadian fans for scoring the goal. Like Henderson, there is a famous photograph of Sittler celebrating the goal. There is another interesting picture of Sittler celebrating a few moments later. An impromptu jersey exchange with the Czechoslovakians created a confusing image when Sittler, wearing the number 25 of Bohuslav Ebermann, was proudly waving the Canadian flag.

The famous goal and the resulting glory should not overshadow Sittler's contributions to Team Canada in other areas. He and great friend Lanny McDonald earned great applause for willingly accepting the blue-collar roles assigned to them in that Canada Cup, and he excelled at it, as only Bobby Hull scored more goals for Canada. He was the only Canadian forward named to the tournament all-star team. Also, Sittler would don the Team Canada jersey twice more in his career. In 1982 he represented Canada at the world hockey championships where he scored four goals and seven points in ten contests. He would return to the world championships in 1983, this time picking up a bronze medal thanks in part to his three-goal contribution.

Here is an interesting and little known fact: In 1984 Sittler had special permission from the Philadelphia Flyers to miss the beginning stages of training camp in order to do colour commentary for CTV for the 1984 Canada Cup. To prepare for the NHL season, Sittler practiced with Team Canada. In some respects he was an unofficial member of the victorious 1984 Canada Cup squad.

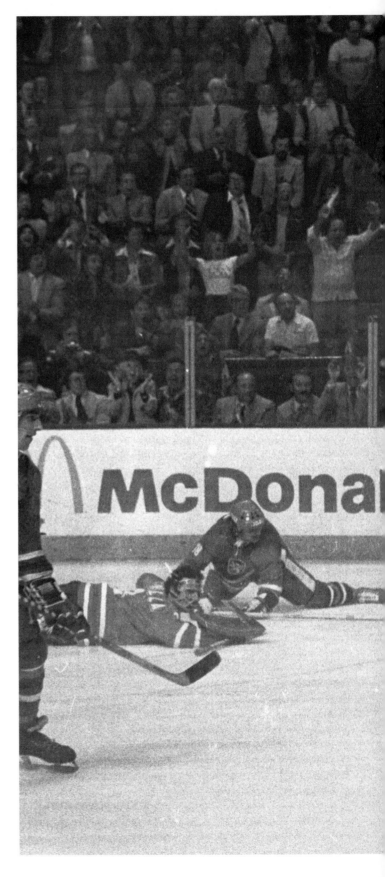

Darryl Sittler

DARRYL SITTLER — *Kitchener, Ontario*

Tournament	GP	G	A	Pts	PIM
1976 Canada Cup	7	4	2	6	4
1982 World Championships	10	4	3	7	2
1983 World Championships	10	3	1	4	12
Team Canada Totals	27	11	6	17	18

Darryl Sittler wheels away in celebration after scoring the winning goal in the 1976 Canada Cup.

Gordie Howe

GORDIE HOWE — *Floral, Saskatchewan*

Tournament	GP	G	A	Pts	PIM
1974 Summit Series	7	3	4	7	2
Team Canada Totals	21	4	17	21	34

Gordie Howe battles with Gennady Tsygankov near Vladislav Tretiak's goal during the 1974 WHA Summit Series with the Soviet Union. Right: Howe turns to watch Tretiak smother a deflected shot on goal.

WHILE THE 1972 SUMMIT SERIES IS THE MOST CELEBRATED INTERNATIONAL hockey tournament of all time, not a lot of people realize there was a second Summit Series.

In 1974, the World Hockey Association, a new rival to the National Hockey League, decided to capitalize on the thirst for another Soviet-Canada showdown. They quenched that thirst by creating their own version of Team Canada and by creating a copycat Summit Series tournament.

The WHA even brought in several 1972 stars that had since defected to the upstart league. Back were Paul Henderson, Pat Stapleton, and Frank Mahovlich. This time Bobby Hull was included. Another name added to the roster was hockey's ultimate legend – Gordie Howe.

Arguably the greatest hockey player of all time, Howe had retired prior to the 1972 Summit Series. He had come out of retirement in order to join the WHA's Houston Aeros where his sons Mark and Marty played. Both of his sons joined their father for the WHA version of Team Canada despite their American birth certificates.

Howe's inclusion piqued interest in the tournament. Canadians were well aware of the great Soviet players by this time. How could the forty-six-year-old living legend perform against the likes of speedy Valery Kharlamov, Boris Mikhailov, and Alexander Maltsev?

Howe never had any concern. In his first season out of retirement he scored 100 points, was named WHA MVP and led the Aeros to the Avco Cup championship. He was excited to get a chance to play against the Soviets. Though he had proved he could still play at an elite level at his advanced age, there were many doubters.

Howe quickly quieted his critics. He excelled on a line with Ralph Backstrom at centre and son Mark on left wing. The trio formed Canada's top line. Howe produced three goals and seven points in seven games. He played in all situations including the power play and the penalty kill, and was on the ice for almost every crucial situation Team Canada encountered.

One reason the '74 Summit is not well remembered is the apparently poor performance by Team Canada: records indicate that the team won only a single game against the Soviets that year. But a closer analysis suggests they were simply unlucky not to have done better. Canada got off to a surprising 1-0-1 start after the first two games, but bad coaching decisions cost them Game Three and a commanding series lead. The two teams tied Game Four, a game Howe was dominant in. With a little more puck-luck, Howe could have won the game himself. The Soviets took control of the series back in Moscow, but may have literally stolen victory from Canada's hands in Game Seven. The timekeeper mysteriously allowed a few precious seconds to disappear late in the game. A second or so after the final whistle blew, Canada scored to win the game. The goal was disallowed. Canada went 1-4-3 in the tournament, but could easily have been 4-4.

Howe was extremely impressed by the Soviets, saying, "They just played too damn good," at the end of the series.

The Soviets, too, were simply awestruck by Howe. Prior to 1972, the Soviets had always heard tales of Rocket Richard, Jean Beliveau, Bobby Hull, Bobby Orr, and Gordie Howe, but had never faced any of them until 1974. It is interesting that even the Soviets gave Howe and Hull that little bit of extra respect reserved for the game's true legends.

The Soviets were especially impressed with the high skill level Howe still displayed at such an advanced age. The Soviets had always believed players should focus on coaching younger players once they passed the age of thirty. Seeing Howe's incredible talents at age forty-six made them think twice about forcing top players off their national team because of their age.

Mike Bossy

ONE OF THE MAIN REASONS MIKE BOSSY IS CONSIDERED BY MANY TO BE THE GREATEST GOAL SCORER IN HOCKEY history was his ability to seemingly always score the big goal in the big games. The New York Islanders right-winger scored 573 career NHL goals in just 752 games, and added an impressive 85 goals in just 129 playoff games. He collected four Stanley Cups and practically every individual award along the way.

With those credentials, Bossy was an obvious choice to represent Canada in international events. Bossy would get that prestigious opportunity only twice, and both times he would assert himself as a Canadian goal-scoring hero.

Bossy endured a short summer in 1981. Having gone deep into the NHL playoffs to capture the Islanders' second consecutive Stanley Cup, Bossy was a key inclusion on the 1981 Canada Cup team that September. Bossy was joined by Islanders linemates Bryan Trottier and Clark Gillies to form Team Canada's second line in that tournament, playing behind a "Dream Line" of Gilbert Perreault, Wayne Gretzky, and Guy Lafleur. In just seven games the "Islanders Line" combined for twenty-nine points. Bossy led the entire tournament with eight goals, and was only one point behind Gretzky for the scoring championship. Everything was going perfectly for Canada — too perfectly. The Soviet Union blitzed Canada 8-1 in the winner-take-all championship game.

Not wanting to leave that sour taste in his mouth, Bossy returned to Team Canada for the 1984 Canada Cup. It was not an easy decision for Bossy, however. His Islanders had just relinquished the Stanley Cup championship for the first time since 1980. His ace linemate Bryan Trottier, a dual citizen, opted to play for the United States instead of Canada in this tournament. And Bossy, who was already irritable because of a late-summer decision to quit smoking, had hurt his knee just prior to training camp. But Bossy persevered, and Canadian hockey fans are forever grateful.

Though Trottier and Gillies were not there, Bossy headlined a new Islanders Line for Canada Cup '84. The unit of Bossy, John Tonelli, and Brent Sutter proved to be a tremendously successful combination, as Tonelli went on to win MVP honours and the line scored twenty-two points in eight games and Sutter established himself as an elite player.

Bossy scored five goals and nine points in eight games that September, but none of his goals were more important than the one he scored during the Canada Cup semi-final contest between Canada and the Soviet Union.

At 12:29 into overtime, Bossy capped off one of the most memorable and exciting plays in Canada Cup history. He expertly redirected a Paul Coffey shot past screened Soviet goalie Vladimir Myshkin. Seconds earlier, Soviet forwards Vladimir Kovin and Mikhail Varnakov threatened to score on a two-on-one, but the play was broken up incredibly by Paul Coffey. Coffey quickly went into attack mode and penetrated the Soviet zone. The Islanders Line went to work and got the puck back to Coffey. Coffey expertly fired a shot with the full intention of allowing Bossy to deflect it for one of the most famous goals in Canadian hockey history.

The Canadian win was sweet revenge for the humiliating loss suffered three years earlier in that same tournament against the Soviets. The victory knocked the U.S.S.R. out of the tournament, and advanced Canada to the finals against Sweden, in which they captured their second Canada Cup championship with relative ease.

Injuries ended Bossy's career prematurely in the summer of 1987. In addition to several lost years of NHL dominance, hockey fans were unable to see Bossy return to the Canada Cup in 1987. No doubt if Bossy's back had not given out on him, he would have been one of the top scorers and overall players in 1987.

Those who were fortunate enough to see Bossy skate in a Canadian uniform have to agree that he was one of the all-time greats to represent his country. He did it with determination, and lots of goals.

MIKE BOSSY — *Montreal, Quebec*

Tournament	GP	G	A	Pts	PIM
1981 Canada Cup	7	8	3	11	2
1984 Canada Cup	8	5	4	9	2
Team Canada Totals	15	13	7	20	4

Mike Bossy tips the puck past Soviet goalie Vladimir Myshkin to win the semi-final of the 1984 Canada Cup.

John Tonelli

JOHN TONELLI RANKS AS ONE OF THE ALL-TIME GREAT grinders. Built like a truck, Tonelli loved to dig for loose pucks in the corners and along the boards. While his strength and smarts helped him win more battles than he lost, it was his ability to make a play with the puck once he retrieved it that truly made him a valuable contributor to any team he played on.

Tonelli certainly had a knack for showing up big in the crucial games. This was especially evident in Stanley Cup playoff competition. When his New York Islanders captured their first Stanley Cup title in 1980, it was his overtime pass to Bob Nystrom that dramatically clinched the victory. In 1982 Tonelli scored back-to-back game-winning goals when the Islanders tied and surpassed the old NHL team record for the longest unbeaten streak in the playoffs. Tonelli also enabled the Islanders to come back against Pittsburgh in the fifth and deciding game of the playoff series with both a game-tying and OT game-winning goal. That eventually paved the way for the Islanders' third straight Stanley Cup win.

Tonelli's reputation and track record as a big game player made him an obvious choice to play for Team Canada in the 1984 Canada Cup. Surprised by the invitation, Tonelli almost turned down the training camp offer because he did not think he was likely to make the final cut. But make the team he did, and he became a legend of Canadian hockey.

Tonelli's contagious enthusiasm on and off the ice quickly rubbed off on his inspired teammates. He put in one of the finest performances in Canada Cup history, as he showed up every night wearing his heart on his sleeve and deservingly walked away with the tournament Most Valuable Player award.

Playing on an all–New York Islander line with Brent Sutter and Mike Bossy, Tonelli set the tone early in the series by being voted Canada's best player in a 7-2 game against Czechoslovakia.

He duplicated the feat in the semi-final classic against the Soviets. In that game Tonelli opened the scoring and assisted on Mike Bossy's thrilling overtime winning goal. In the two-game finals against Sweden, Tonelli picked up a goal and an assist in the first game to finish the tournament with three goals and nine points in eight games.

Tonelli was not named the tournament's MVP because of his scoring statistics. In true Tonelli style — in true Canadian style — his contributions to the team's success were not readily measurable by any statistic. It was his leadership-by-example and his gung-ho style and work ethic that propelled an at-times lethargic Team Canada '84 to the Canada Cup championship.

Tonelli's only Team Canada appearance was memorable. In every major tournament Team Canada looks for hardworking role players who will put in a gritty effort to gain an edge on the opposition. These role players are often the stereotypical Canadians and a major reason for Team Canada's many successes over the years. Tonelli's legendary performance in the 1984 Canada Cup is the perfect example of this.

JOHN TONELLI — *Milton, Ontario*

Tournament	GP	G	A	Pts	PIM
1984 Canada Cup	8	3	6	9	2
Team Canada Totals	8	3	6	9	2

John Tonelli's emotional play was an inspiration to Team Canada during the 1984 Canada Cup. At left, he celebrates with teammate Paul Coffey. Above, letting it all hang out after a goal against archrival the Soviet Union.

Brent Sutter

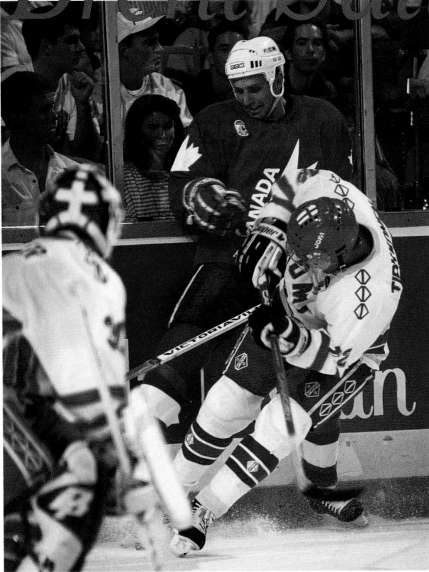

BRENT SUTTER — *Viking, Alberta*

Tournament	GP	G	A	Pts	PIM
1984 Canada Cup	8	2	2	4	10
1986 World Championships	8	4	7	11	8
1987 Canada Cup	9	1	3	4	6
1991 Canada Cup	8	3	1	4	6
Team Canada Totals	33	10	13	23	30

Brent Sutter made a living out of tenacious checking and gritty two-way play. Images on these pages show him in action during the 1991 Canada Cup against Finland (left) and Russia.

MEMBERS OF THE SUTTER FAMILY OF VIKING, ALBERTA, ARE UNIQUE legends in Canadian hockey. Six brothers all achieved the Canadian dream by making it to the National Hockey League. And they all personified several key attributes of Canadian hockey such as heart, determination, and desire over physical skill.

Despite their legendary intangibles, only one brother, Brent, would play for Team Canada when all of the nation's best were available to participate. Brian did participate in five World Junior Championship games in 1975, while Ron participated in the 1990 World Championships. But only Brent was deemed to be among Canada's absolute best when he was chosen to play in three Canada Cup tournaments.

Brent's debut in a Team Canada jersey came in the 1984 Canada Cup, and might very well have come at the expense of brother Brian. Brent was one of the last players to make the team, while Brian was one of the last to be cut. Interestingly, even though Brent had three seasons and two Stanley Cup championships on his résumé, it was not until he made Team Canada that he truly believed he belonged as an elite player.

Sutter centred one of the team's key lines with fellow New York Islander teammates Mike Bossy and John Tonelli as wingers. Sutter chipped in with two goals and two assists, but it was the typical Sutter guts and sacrifice that endeared him to all hockey fans coast to coast.

Sutter made such an impression on Team Canada's brass in 1984 that he was invited back in 1987, and he was never better than in that Canada Cup. Everyone remembers the incredible scoring dramatics of Wayne Gretzky and Mario Lemieux, but it was the great play of many role players, led by the Kamikaze combination of Sutter and Rick Tocchet, that helped Canada edge out the Soviet Union in the most thrilling Canada Cup final of all.

Coach Mike Keenan loved the work ethic of Sutter, and somewhat surprisingly named the veteran to the 1991 Canada Cup team. The team, dubbed "Mike [Keenan] and the Mechanics" or "Gretzky and the Grinders," became the only team in Canada Cup history to go through the entire tournament undefeated. A big part of that success was Sutter, who led the lunch-pailers with three goals in eight games.

In addition to his top-level international experience, Brent also represented Canada in the 1986 World Championships, scoring four goals and eleven points in eight contests. Although the NHL usually kept him busy in the spring, this rare opportunity to help Team Canada at the world championships is a cherished item on Sutter's list of accomplishments.

For all of his immeasurable efforts that resulted in three championships in a Team Canada jersey, Brent Sutter has certainly earned his place among Team Canada's all-time legends.

Paul

PAUL COFFEY WAS ONE OF THE GREATEST SKATERS AND offensive players to ever lace on the skates. His effortless moves and uncanny ability to create opportunities made him virtually a fourth forward out on the ice, especially during his days with the explosive Edmonton Oilers, but also with Team Canada.

International hockey only emphasized his abilities. He was a pleasure to watch, streaking down the ice, cutting through defences like a hot knife through butter. His skating always looked so smooth and seemingly facile that one wondered if the man had a built-in cruise control and a small rocket engine in his skates. While his feet may have been gifted, his hockey stick was well educated. He was a general of the offence — capable of making breakaway passes or rushing the puck himself.

Coffey wore the Canadian sweater in three Canada Cups, one World Cup, and one World Championship tournament. He collected a total of thirty-eight points in forty-three official games for Canada. His totals include seven goals and thirty-one assists. Only Wayne Gretzky has scored more points in a Team Canada uniform in Canada Cup/World Cup history.

Although overshadowed by Gretzky and Mario Lemieux, Coffey had a magnificent 1987 Canada Cup, scoring two goals and six points. Not many people realize that Coffey was the fifth player on the ice when Canada scored the dramatic tournament-winning goal. Everyone remembers Lemieux scoring on a pass from Gretzky. Many people remember Dale Hawerchuk winning the initial faceoff to start the play, and defenceman Larry Murphy jumping up to make it a three on one. Coffey uncharacteristically stayed behind to play defence.

In 1991 Coffey and Mark Messier picked up the slack when Gretzky was felled by a back injury. Coffey led all defencemen in scoring with seven points. And in 1996, Coffey added another seven points, sharing the defenceman scoring title with USA's Brian Leetch. In

fact, Coffey tied with Gretzky for the Team Canada scoring lead, and finished tied for third in scoring overall.

Ironically, Coffey's greatest offensive output happened in his first tour with Team Canada — in the 1984 Canada Cup. Coffey scored three goals and eleven points in eight games. That ranked him as the highest-scoring defenceman in the tournament, and tied for second in overall scoring, behind only Gretzky.

I say ironically because, for all of his great offence generated while in a Team Canada uniform, it is odd that his most famous moment was a crucial defensive play in the 1984 Canada Cup that is still etched in the minds of many.

The play happened in the semi-final thriller against the Soviets. The two teams were tied at two goals apiece and battling for the win in overtime. At the twelve-minute mark two Soviet forwards, Vladimir Kovin and Mikhail Varnakov, broke in on a two-on-one situation against Coffey. Kovin tried to flip a pass over to Varnakov, but Coffey read the play perfectly and broke up the pass with his stick. Then Coffey did what he did best — he just turned on the afterburners, leaving the two Soviet forwards well behind him in the Canadian zone. Coffey zoomed towards the Soviet zone and got the puck in deep. Canadian forechecker John Tonelli regained the puck and put it back to the point. Coffey picked up the pass and fired a shot on goal, where Mike Bossy managed to redirect the shot into the net for a famous victory. It was a sweet win for the Canadians, who avenged the humiliating defeat by the Soviets from three years earlier.

While the win ensured Canada would advance, and Canada would go on to knock off Sweden in the finals, everybody who saw this famous Canada-U.S.S.R. tilt knew it was the true championship game. Coffey was a huge contributor to the victory, doing it in a surprising manner with a great defensive play. In fact, he played so well during that 1984 Canada Cup tournament that he made his only international All-Star team.

Coffey

One of the most gifted skaters to ever play for Canada, Paul Coffey's offensive skills earned him almost a point a game for Canada. Above and left are images of Coffey on the prowl during the 1991 Canada Cup.

PAUL COFFEY — *Weston, Ontario*

Tournament	GP	G	A	Pts	PIM
1984 Canada Cup	8	3	8	11	4
1987 Canada Cup	9	2	4	6	0
1990 World Championships	10	1	6	7	10
1991 Canada Cup	8	1	6	7	8
1996 World Cup of Hockey	8	0	7	7	12
Team Canada Totals	43	7	31	38	34

Wayne Gretzky

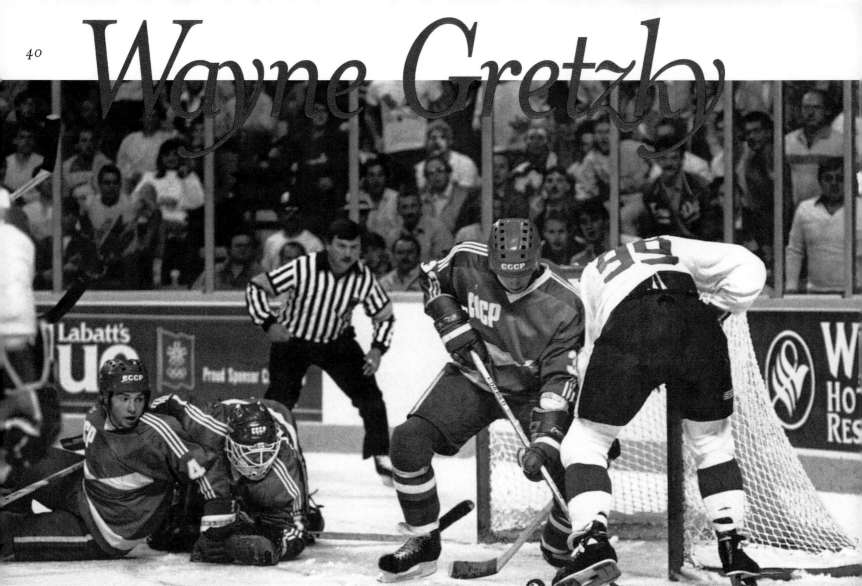

WHEN HE RETIRED, WAYNE GRETZKY WAS asked which team he wanted to be remembered playing for — the Edmonton Oilers or the Los Angeles Kings. Using his typical diplomacy to deflect the question, Gretzky smugly replied, "Team Canada."

It may have been a deft stickhandling manoeuvre through a tough question, but it very well could be a legitimate answer. Gretzky participated in the world junior championships, the world championships, the World Cup of Hockey, and the Olympics.

But it was Gretzky's involvement in four of the five Canada Cup tournaments that will always be remembered first and foremost when it comes to the Great One's Team Canada involvement. Like virtually every other level of hockey he participated in, "The Great One" dominated the Canada Cup.

His story is well documented. He did not particularly enjoy the 1981 tournament. He felt the team was poorly run and his own play "stunk." Canada's humiliating failure in the 8-1 loss to the Soviets in the final only added extra ammunition to the anti-Gretzky faction who said, "Sure he can score, but he can't win." For the next couple of years many of his mind-boggling scoring accomplishments were dismissed due to a lack of team success.

The 1984 Canada Cup was much sweeter. The Oilers had just come off their first Stanley Cup and now seemingly half of that team would represent Team Canada in the Canada Cup. Gretzky would help lead Canada to victory, though he described the win as "anti-climatic," since the Soviets were not in the final.

The 1987 tournament featured Wayne Gretzky in his absolute prime. Despite some pre-tournament noise about himz sitting out and rest-

ing his weary body from the long NHL season and playoffs, Wayne showed up and, together with a young phenom named Mario Lemieux, put on the show of a lifetime. The Soviets gave Team Canada everything they had in the most exciting multi-game final in international hockey history. But in the end — actually 1:34 away from the end — Gretzky and Lemieux teamed up one last time to score the tournament-winning goal. Gretzky himself has said time and again that he has never played better hockey than he did in the 1987 Canada Cup.

The 1991 edition was a different Canada Cup for Gretzky. By this time he had been traded to Los Angeles and many believed he had been unseated as the world's best hockey player by Lemieux. Others were saying Mark Messier and Steve Yzerman were also nearly equal to an aging Great One. Though Mario missed the tournament with an injury,

Gretzky, flanked by a great supporting cast, put on a display of hockey that convincingly reaffirmed his status atop the hockey world.

It should come as no surprise that he is the all-time leading scorer in Canada Cup history. In thirty-one games he amassed seventeen goals and forty assists for fifty-seven points. He leads his closest rival, Sergei Makarov of Russia, by twenty-six points. And that does not even include the three goals and seven points he got as a

Nagano Games featured the first Olympic tournament open to all NHL professionals. Because of the NHL season, the Olympics were the only major hockey tournament that Wayne had never participated in. However, Gretzky would leave Japan with bitter memories. The Czech Republic, backed by goalie Dominik Hasek, Canada's greatest single nemesis since Russia's Vladislav Tretiak, battled Team Canada to a 1-1 draw after regulation and extra time. The game would be decided in a

Wayne Gretzky — *Brantford, Ontario*

Tournament	GP	G	A	Pts	PIM
1978 World Juniors	6	8	9	17	2
1981 Canada Cup	7	5	7	12	2
1982 World Championships	10	6	8	14	0
1984 Canada Cup	8	5	7	12	2
1987 Canada Cup	9	3	18	21	2
1991 Canada Cup	7	4	8	12	2
1996 World Cup of Hockey	8	3	4	7	2
1998 Olympic Games	6	0	4	4	2
Team Canada Totals	61	34	65	99	14

Left: Gretzky attacks the Soviet goal during the 1987 Canada Cup. This page, centre: Gretzky hammers a slapshot at the Soviet goal during the 1991 Canada Cup. Top and bottom: images from the 1991 Cup and 1998 Olympics.

thirty-six-year-old in the 1996 World Cup of Hockey. By this time he was a shadow of his former self, yet still better than most in the world. Gretzky once again proved all his critics wrong.

There is no doubting that the Canada Cup tourneys hold a special place in Wayne's vast collection of hockey memories. Here's what he wrote in his autobiography:

"Winning the Stanley Cup is a sweet, sweet feeling, and when you win it, you don't believe anything can match it. But winning that Canada Cup is every bit as sweet in a different way. We get paid millions of dollars to do our best for the NHL, but we play the Canada Cup for our country and for our players' association and for the love of the game. And when you do it for those reasons, and you play those reasons, and you play the hardest and best hockey of your life, the payoff seems pure and lasting and unforgettable."

As gifted a wordsmith as he is a hockey player, Wayne Gretzky perfectly summed up what the Canada Cup was all about.

In 1998, the Great One got his first chance to have similar experiences at the Olympic Games. The

shootout, with Gretzky sitting on the bench. The Czechs would go on to win that game and the gold medal. Canada would play for bronze but put in a disappointing effort against Finland. Gretzky would go home without any Olympic medal at all.

By the time the 2002 Salt Lake City Olympics came around, Gretzky had already retired. But he returned to Team Canada in a major capacity. He headed the men's hockey team, selecting the coaches, the managerial staff, and of course the players. Just like he always was on the ice, Gretzky was still a key Team Canada figure off it.

You know the rest of the story: Canada would stumble through the round robin and be fired up by a Gretzky public rant. And with a little luck from a loonie imbedded at centre ice, Canada would go on to capture Olympic gold for the first time in fifty years.

Gretzky did not officially get a gold medal, as only players receive that honour. But he was very much a part of that championship. His involvement as a manager at the Olympics and his return to the position for the 2004 World Cup of Hockey only underlines his undeniable status as the ultimate legend of Team Canada.

Mario Lemieux

MARIO LEMIEUX — *Montreal, Quebec*

Tournament	GP	G	A	Pts	PIM
1983 World Juniors	7	5	5	10	12
1985 World Championships	9	4	6	10	2
1987 Canada Cup	9	11	7	18	8
2002 Olympic Games	5	2	4	6	0
2004 World Cup Of Hockey	6	1	4	5	2
Team Canada Totals	36	23	26	49	24

ONE OF THE GREATEST THINGS ABOUT THE 1987 CANADA CUP WAS THAT we got to see Mario Lemieux achieve his potential. For it was in that tournament that he arrived in the same stratosphere of hockey stardom as Wayne Gretzky.

Ever since he was a teenager, Lemieux had had everyone drooling over his ability. He had the size and natural skills that Gretzky could only dream of. If there ever was a player who could catch some of Gretzky's scoring records, it was Mario.

Early in his career, Lemieux languished with the lowly Pittsburgh Penguins. The team seemed to just accept defeat many nights. Without great leadership, it looked like Mario might never learn what it would take to harness his potential, and until that happened the Penguins would never develop into a great team. And Mario, despite wondrous natural abilities matched only by perhaps Bobby Orr, might never have developed into the great player he became.

That all changed at the 1987 Canada Cup. And as a result, Lemieux's career and the fortunes of the Pittsburgh Penguins changed, too.

No one — not Mark Messier or Dale Hawerchuk and especially not Gretzky, as many people think — physically took Mario aside in that tournament and taught him how to win. Just by being in the same atmosphere as such leaders and by watching and noting what these superstars did to prepare themselves and their team for victory, Lemieux learned what it would take to achieve his potential and be a winner.

Mario began to emulate their work ethic and commitment, and as the tournament went on, he was rewarded with greatness. He ended up scoring eleven goals in just nine games. The eleven goals is a single-tournament record. Despite playing in just the one tournament, his eleven goals ranks fifth on the all-time Canada Cup goal-scoring leader board. His eighteen points were bettered only by Gretzky's twenty-one in the same tourney for a single-tournament best. That one-tournament outburst ranks Lemieux eighth on the all-time scoring list, despite playing in far fewer games than most of the others.

More important, Lemieux scored both game-winning goals for Canada in the best-of-three finale against the Soviets. Both rank among the most famous goals of all time. In Game Two he snapped up a cross-crease pass from Gretzky to end a two-overtime marathon. And we all know what happened in Game Three. With a little over a minute left he took a soft drop pass from Gretzky and put the puck over Sergei Mylnikov's glove to clinch the championship. Only Paul Henderson's heroic 1972 Summit Series goal ranks higher in the memories of Canadians.

"To have the opportunity to be on the same team as Wayne — especially the last two games to play on his right side — is going to stay with me the rest of my life. To have a chance to play with the greatest player in the world, somebody I looked up to my whole career, it was incredible to be part of it with him," reminisced Lemieux years later.

It certainly did stay with him. Lemieux became an unstoppable offensive force that would win two Stanley Cups. The only thing that could slow down Mario the Magnificent was his health. Serious injuries, such as a chronic bad back, coupled with a bout of Hodgkin's disease (a form of cancer) would cause Lemieux to miss much playing time during the 1990s, including all opportunities to represent Canada internationally. Mario turned down chances to play in the 1991 Canada Cup and 1996 World Cup of Hockey, and had officially retired several months before the opening up of the Olympic Games to NHL professionals in 1998.

Three years into retirement Mario rediscovered his love for the game. Completely healthy, Mario would make a legendary comeback in 2000–2001, taking the NHL by storm.

The 2001–2002 season was not as smooth-sailing for Mario. He had developed a chronic hip condition that limited him to only six goals in twenty-four games and would eventually cost him the remainder of the NHL season. Lemieux, now also an owner of the Penguins team, put his own team's fortunes behind his personal aspirations as he was motivated by the opportunity to once again play for Team Canada — this time at the 2002 Olympic Winter Games in Salt Lake City, Utah.

Even at less than one hundred percent health, Lemieux proved he was still the best player in the world. And as team captain, Lemieux was

determined to lead Canada back to Olympic gold medal glory for the first time in fifty years.

The rest of the story will one day be as legendary as Lemieux himself. Lemieux was instrumental in the round robin game against the Czech Republic. Czech goalie Dominik Hasek had had Canadian sharpshooters snake-bitten for several years, but he had never faced off against Lemieux in that time. Lemieux scored twice in a 3-3 round robin tie to lift the proverbial monkey off the Canadians' backs.

That game really helped the Canadians turn around what had been a lacklustre Olympic showing to that point. The Canadians got better and better and wound up in the gold medal game against the hosts, Team USA.

There were many great performances in that gold medal game, including Lemieux's. He made the play of the tournament when he let an intended pass to him go through his legs, much to the surprise of the American defencemen and goalie. The puck, as Lemieux fully knew, would continue past to a streaking Paul Kariya, who would bury it in behind American goalie Mike Richter.

Later on Lemieux inexplicably missed what should have been the gold medal–clinching goal as he rang the shot off the goal post. Though he was more shocked than anyone, it turned out to be a moot point, as Canada would go on to capture Olympic gold by a score of 5-2.

"This was the chance of a lifetime, to play in the Olympics. To do something great for your country is awesome," said the proud Canadian captain.

Lemieux would return for another great Canadian moment in 2004. Though injuries limited him to just ten games in the 2003–2004 season, he proved he is still among the world's best at the 2004 World Cup of Hockey. He scored one goal and five points, and at times reminded us of the Mario of old. He really impressed as a leader and a defensive presence.

The 2004 World Cup was the completion of Mario Lemieux's evolution as a legend of Team Canada. In 1987 he was the young gun to whom the torch had been passed and who led Canada to victory. In 2004, he was the one passing the torch to the next generation of Canadian hockey legends — including the likes of Vincent Lecavalier, Joe Thornton, and Brad Richards.

Above left: Lemieux rips the winning goal over Sergei Mylnikov's glove as Canada wins the 1987 Canada Cup. At right, he fights through the stick check of Soviet forward Valery Kamensky.

WHENEVER SOMEONE DESCRIBES MARK Messier, the term "leadership" always comes to the forefront. And well it should. He was the emotional and physical leader of the dynastic Edmonton Oilers, even when good buddy Wayne Gretzky was the official captain. Once Gretzky went to Hollywood, Messier led the Oilers back to the Stanley Cup championship just two seasons later. His legendary status as one of pro sport's great leaders was cemented in 1994 when he guided the New York Rangers to the Stanley Cup — Manhattan's first in fifty-four years!

So it should come as no surprise that when you think of Mark Messier's play in the Canada Cups, his leadership stands out first and foremost. The three-time Canada Cup champion was instrumental in both the 1984 and 1987 Canadian victories. He took a back seat to the likes of Gretzky, Lemieux, and Coffey, but his fearless play and win-at-all-costs attitude intimidated the Soviets and all other nations.

In the 1984 Canada Cup, the Soviets sent a more physical lineup to battle, led by Vladimir Kovin. It was Messier who delivered the message right back at the Soviets, re-arranging Kovin's face in a famous (or perhaps infamous) stick carving incident.

In the 1987 Canada Cup, Messier's line was most often matched up against the famed Soviet Green Unit — the KLM Line of Krutov, Larionov, and Makarov. Messier shut down Larionov in particular, and by doing so he showed his teammates that he was willing to sacrifice goals and assists for the good of the team. Everyone else on Team Canada noticed and followed suit. Even superstars like Dale Hawerchuk and Michel Goulet gladly accepted lesser roles. Team Canada was much stronger because of this example of Messier's leadership.

"Mark was very instrumental in bringing that group together," said Canadian head coach Mike Keenan. "How Mark impacted his team was incredible. In Game Two in 1987, we were tied after regulation. He came in and just jacked the room right up. It was really an incredible experience. And the team stayed jacked up, even more so for Game Three. Honest to God, you could feel the energy in the room, like I've never experienced in any situation before or after. The energy was so high, it was like they were walking on air after he spoke."

Mark Messier

The 1991 Canada Cup was a tough tournament for Messier personally. Due to injuries, he missed the entire training camp and was not expected to play at all. Then, on the last day of camp, he limped in and was named to the team. He played a quiet and largely ineffective role, but would be ready when the team really needed him to be.

And the team did need him. Wayne Gretzky, clearly the tournament's best player, was crunched from behind by USA defender Gary Suter. The hit left "The Great One" unable to play in what proved to be the decisive game. The loss of Gretzky could have proved deadly for Team Canada, but Messier, along with Paul Coffey, took the proverbial bull by the horns and kept the team confident and focused. Messier himself scored the all-important goal in the third period of Game One to calm the team down, then opened the scoring in Game Two. Despite his injuries, Messier was dominant when the time came for him to be.

Mark Messier is one of hockey's all-time greatest players and, not surprisingly, one of Team Canada's greatest heroes. If it were possible to create an all-Canadian dream team comprising players from all eras, Mark Messier would be included, and would be the leader. Like many of Canada's all-time greats, his inclusion is not determined by goals and assists but rather by impact and intangible qualities.

MARK MESSIER — *Edmonton, Alberta*

Tournament	GP	G	A	Pts	PIM
1984 Canada Cup	8	2	4	6	8
1987 Canada Cup	9	1	6	7	6
1989 World Championships	6	3	3	6	8
1991 Canada Cup	8	2	6	8	10
1996 World Cup of Hockey	7	1	4	5	12
Team Canada Totals	38	9	23	32	44

Always one of Canada's most physical players, Messier rocks USA's Brett Hull as they duel during the 1991 Canada Cup.
Left: Messier at work during the 1996 World Cup.

Before 1987, Dale Hawerchuk was labelled a one-way scoring machine that could not quite lead his team to NHL post-season success. That label changed forever with the 1987 Canada Cup.

Hawerchuk was a brilliant centre with the Winnipeg Jets in the 1980s. Had it not been for Wayne Gretzky in Edmonton, Hawerchuk quite possibly could have been known as the best offensive centre in the game during that decade. He scored over a hundred points in seven of his first eight NHL seasons, including an incredible 1984–85 season when he scored 53 goals and 130 points. But Hawerchuk's Jets could never find NHL post-season success, often because of Gretzky's Oilers. It seemed to be a rite of spring in Manitoba — the Jets losing to the Oilers in the first round of the playoffs.

Hawerchuk, who had previously represented Canada in the 1981 World Junior Championships and the 1982 and 1986 World Championships (winning bronze medals each time), was finally able to join Gretzky and company on the same team in 1987 when he was named to Team Canada for the Canada Cup. But it meant Hawerchuk would have to change his game.

For all the accolades he'd earned for his offence skills, it was Hawerchuk's willingness to accept a lesser role in the Canada Cup that often earns him the most praise. On Team Canada Hawerchuk was ready to be a support player rather than the go-to guy. He played fewer minutes, and concentrated more on defensive play and the finer points of the game such as faceoffs and leadership. His selflessness inspired teammates who were in a similar situation, and as a result he played a significant role in the memorable 1987 victory.

His dedication to excellence was most notable in the final goal of the tournament. While everyone remembers the famous Gretzky-to-Lemieux goal to capture victory, not everyone remembers that it was Hawerchuk who won the all-important draw deep in the Canadian end to start that play. While Gretzky and Lemieux went down-ice to immortalize the tournament as the greatest hockey ever played, Hawerchuk gave Valeri Kamensky an undetected neutral zone tug to ensure the odd-man rush for Canada. Hawerchuk was fortunate there was no penalty on the play, but the euphoria of the goal and subsequent victory, combined with his gritty leadership and play, ensured Hawerchuk's status as a legend.

Hawerchuk returned to his offensive leader role when he next played for Team Canada in 1989. With the Jets out of the playoffs, Hawerchuk returned to the World Championships and scored four goals and twelve points in ten games as Canada captured the silver medal.

Hawerchuk would return for his final appearance in the red and white jersey of Team Canada in 1991 for the final edition of the Canada Cup. Under the guidance of returning coach Mike Keenan, Hawerchuk reprised his 1987 assignment as role player extraordinaire. He chipped in five points as Canada breezed to another Canada Cup victory.

Playing for Team Canada often requires stars to assume lesser roles for the betterment of the team. Dale Hawerchuk exhibited that more than anyone, and as a result he is a true legend of Team Canada.

Dale Hawerchuk follows through on a scoring try against American goalie Mike Richter as defenceman Dave Christian moves in to help during the 1991 Canada Cup.

Dale

Hawerchuk

DALE HAWERCHUK — *Toronto, Ontario*

Tournament	GP	G	A	Pts	PIM
1981 World Juniors	5	5	4	9	2
1982 World Championships	10	3	1	4	0
1986 World Championships	8	2	4	6	4
1987 Canada Cup	9	4	2	6	0
1989 World Championships	10	4	8	12	6
1991 Canada Cup	8	2	3	5	0
Team Canada Totals	50	20	22	42	12

Raymond Bourque

THERE WAS ALWAYS AN OPEN INVITATION FOR ACE DEFENCEMAN Raymond Bourque to join Team Canada, but there were precious few opportunities to see him perform for his country.

Bourque participated in the NHL playoffs twenty-one times in his twenty-two-year career, so he never had the chance to play for Canada at any of the world championships. But thankfully for Canadian hockey fans, there was the Canada Cup and, later, the Olympics.

Bourque's first appearance with Team Canada came at the 1981 Canada Cup tournament. Only twenty at the time, Bourque was the second-youngest member of Team Canada, with only Wayne Gretzky about a

month younger. During his first two years in the NHL, Bourque had shown tremendous poise and maturity in his play and was already an obvious choice for Team Canada's defence. He lived up to all expectations, trailing only veteran Denis Potvin in points among all defencemen in that tournament. Canada would bow to the Soviets in that competition, but even though the result for Canada was disappointing, the play of the young Bourque was encouraging. It was obvious that in Bourque, Canada had a world-class defenceman for many years to come.

During the 1984 Canada Cup, Bourque took a more defensive role for the collective good of the team. With the likes of Paul Coffey, Doug Wilson, and Larry Robinson on the team, there was little shortage of

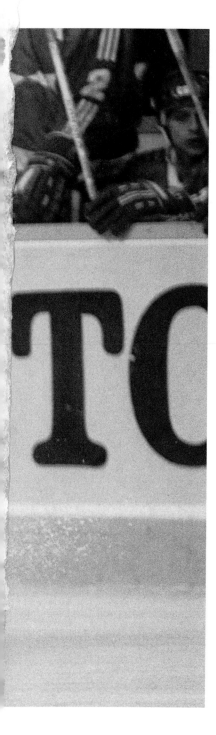

offence from the Canadian blue line. Bourque would see sporadic ice time on the powerplay but his efforts in his own zone were as elite as they were unsung. And ultimately the final outcome was far more gratifying than in 1981. The Canadians got their revenge on the Soviets en route to recapturing the Canada Cup trophy.

Three years later Bourque was once again a shoo-in for Team Canada. Canada and the Soviets met in the best three-game championship series ever played. The end-to-end, fast-paced games were not only a treat for fans all over the world but also the type of hockey environment Bourque thrived in.

When Canada's first powerplay unit stepped on the ice it sent shivers down the spines of hockey aficionados — Gretzky, Lemieux, and Messier as forwards, with Bourque and Coffey on defence.

Bourque had one of the greatest international performances of all time in 1987. He trailed only Gretzky and Lemieux in points on the Canadian team and was the tournament's highest-scoring defenceman with two goals and eight points in nine games. Bourque and Soviet defender Viacheslav Fetisov were named tournament All-Stars.

Left: Ray Bourque wheels into the centre ice area leading a rush against the Russians during the 1987 Canada Cup.

Below: Bourque spills Soviet forward Sergei Makarov.

Bourque, a devoted family man, opted out of the 1991 Canada Cup and 1996 World Cup of Hockey, but returned to Team Canada in 1998 when NHL professionals were welcomed to the Olympic Games. The Olympic experience was unique and exciting for a veteran like Bourque. Bourque was paired with a future teammate named Rob Blake. The duo was dominant, combining for a tournament-best plus eight rating. Bourque added one goal and three points in six Olympic contests, but the shootout loss to the eventual champion Czech Republic was a bitter pill to swallow. Bourque himself missed one of the penalty shots.

Bourque's inclusion as a legend of Team Canada could be debated. Knocks against him include two skipped tournaments and a disappointing ending to his Team Canada career. Additionally, other players in the Canada Cups of the 1980s overshadowed him. But a careful examination of his record confirms his place on the list. His play when he did play was too strong to be overlooked, especially in 1987. And the fact that Canadian hockey fans clamoured for him to play and forgave him when he put his family first indicates just how legendary his contributions to Team Canada were.

RAYMOND BOURQUE — *Montreal, Quebec*

Tournament	GP	G	A	Pts	PIM
1981 Canada Cup	7	1	4	5	6
1984 Canada Cup	8	0	4	4	8
1987 Canada Cup	9	2	6	8	10
1998 Olympics	6	1	2	3	4
Team Canada Totals	30	4	16	20	28

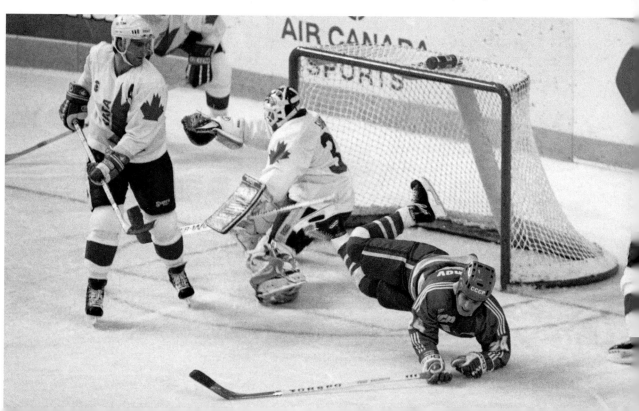

Sean Burke

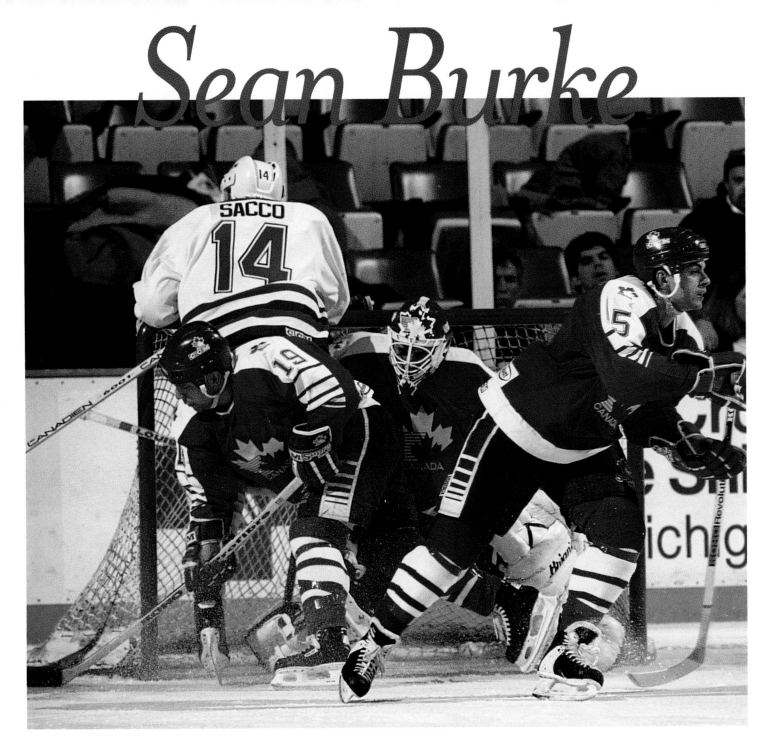

LONG BEFORE HE ESTABLISHED HIMSELF AS A TOP NHL GOALTENDER, Sean Burke was becoming a household name in Canada.

After getting a taste of international hockey in the 1986 World Junior Championships, the highly rated goaltender opted to apprentice with the Canadian national team instead of the minor professional leagues. In the 1986–87 and 1987–88 seasons Burke stopped pucks in seventy-eight official games with the national team, winning forty-six of them. His performance was strong enough to put him on the 1988 Olympic team, though he'd have to share goaltending duties with NHL holdout Andy Moog. They made a formidable tandem, but ultimately the team would finish only in fourth place in front of a Canadian audience.

Burke would go on to the National Hockey League and quickly prove to be a big league netminder. By 1991 his strong play combined with his

international experience made him a solid choice as the third goalie for a victorious Team Canada at the Canada Cup. However, he didn't play a minute of action, as he backed up Bill Ranford and Ed Belfour.

While most of the members of the 1991 Canada Cup championship team quickly disbanded back to their NHL clubs, Burke became involved in a contract dispute with the New Jersey Devils that would ultimately cost him the entire NHL season. Burke returned to his roots and joined the Canadian national team for most of the season. It was perfect timing, as 1992 was another Olympic year. Burke would post a strong 5-2 record with a 2.37 goals against average as he backstopped Canada to an impressive silver medal performance.

Burke frequently played with weak NHL teams and often was knocked out of the playoffs early. As a result he extended his season four times as he participated in as many world championships. Having won silver medals in 1989 and 1991, Burke's 7-1-3 record, including three shutouts, earned him a rare Canadian gold medal at the prestigious tournament in 1997.

Because of his extensive international experience, Burke always seemed to be on the cusp of rejoining Team Canada for major events. Such was the case in 2002 when Ed Belfour edged him out of the reserve goaltender role. Had he made the team, it would have been Burke's third Olympic Games. That would have set a record for Canadian goaltenders and would have tied Terry O'Malley, Wally Schreiber, and Eric Lindros among all hockey players.

Burke returned for his fifth world championships in 2003 and was simply incredible. He was named to the tournament all-star team and named best goalie, as Team Canada rolled through the round robin before squeaking out an overtime win against Sweden in the gold medal game. The tournament would have been perfect for Burke except he aggravated a groin injury and was not able to play in the championship game.

Sean Burke has to be considered one of Team Canada's greatest goaltenders. But that, coupled with his many successes on the international ice surface, does not alone make him a legend. His constant embracing of the international game and of Team Canada at various levels cements it.

Burke had a unique opportunity to become the first NHL player to represent Canada in ten top-level international hockey tournaments. However, politics and his age may play against him. As it stands now he, Eric Lindros, and James Patrick are the only NHLers with nine tournaments, with several at eight. Burke did not play in the 2004 World Cup.

Sean Burke — *Windsor, Ontario*

Tournament	GP	W	L	T	SO	GAA
1986 World Juniors	2	1	1	0	0	3.50
1986-87 Canadian National Team	42	27	13	2	0	3.05
1987 World Championships	5	2	2	1	0	2.40
1987-88 Canadian National Team	37	19	9	2	1	2.81
1988 Olympics	4	1	2	1	0	3.02
1989 World Championships	5	-	-	-	-	2.18
1991 World Championships	8	5	1	2	0	2.63
1991 Canada Cup	0	0	0	0	0	0.00
1991-92 Canadian National Team	31	18	6	4	1	2.61
1992 Olympics	7	5	2	0	0	2.37
1997 World Championships	11	7	1	3	3	2.17
2003 World Championships	6	4	0	1	1	1.28
Team Canada Totals	158	89	37	16	6	

Opposite page: Burke fights for position as Joe Sacco of the USA crashes the crease.
Above: A pre-Olympic victory over the States brings smiles to Burke and teammate Wally Schreiber.

John Slaney

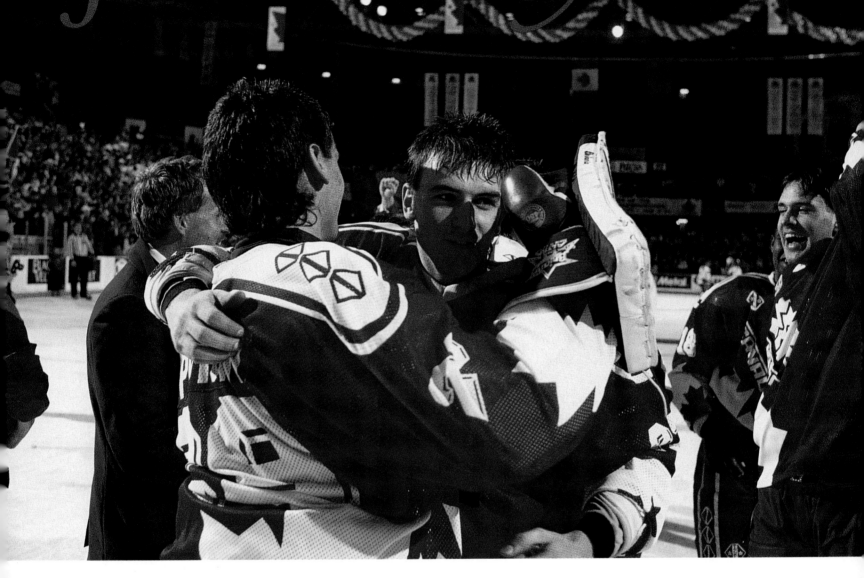

THE WORLD JUNIOR HOCKEY CHAMPIONSHIPS HAVE BECOME CANADIAN hockey fans' favourite annual international tournament. Tuning in to TSN and cheering on our teenaged hockey heroes of tomorrow as they chase the gold is almost as much of a Canadian Christmas-time tradition as mistletoe and stocking stuffers.

Whenever a nation embraces a tournament so fully, fan favourites and national heroes arise almost every year — be it Mike Moller in 1982, Greg Hawgood in 1988, Roberto Luongo in 1999, or Jordin Tootoo in 2003.

Most of the players who represent Team Canada in the illustrious tournament go on to NHL careers, and as a result few are remembered for being a world junior hero once they move on.

One of the rare exceptions to that rule is John Slaney. Slaney was the

unlikeliest of heroes when he scored one of the most famous goals in Team Canada history in 1991. As a result, and despite enjoying a long professional career, his name is forever synonymous with Team Canada.

The 1991 world junior tournament has to rank as one of the best junior tournaments of all time. Saskatchewan fans were treated to four powerhouse teams from Canada, the USA, the Soviet Union, and Czechoslovakia.

Ultimately Team Canada met the Pavel Bure–led Soviets in the final game of the tournament. Canada needed an outright win to capture the gold; the Soviets only needed a tie to clinch the championship.

The phenomenal Eric Lindros headlined a rather anonymous Team Canada that year. Aside from Lindros and defenceman Scott

Niedermayer, it was Slaney who would become a household name in Canada. He did not do it by becoming a NHL superstar, but by scoring the biggest goal of his life.

The teams battled to a 2-2 tie late in the wonderfully played game. Though the tie would have been enough for the U.S.S.R. to win the gold, the Soviets seemed to be taking control of the game late in the contest, when Canada unexpectedly gained the lead.

Slaney, the proud native of St. John's, Newfoundland, took a long shot from the blue line. The shot hit something on its way to the net, as the puck fluttered and eluded Soviet goalie Sergey Zvyagin.

It was an innocent shot, yet so memorable. The Saskatoon fans immediately burst into cheers, as did the rest of the country. Slaney jumped so excitedly that he actually suffered a minor ankle sprain and was not able to play the final few moments. The dramatic win helped make this tournament one of the most memorable in World Junior Hockey Championship history.

Unfortunately, Slaney would not be able to translate his solid junior career and newfound hero status into a regular NHL job. But he would enjoy star status in the minor league levels, as well as 264 sporadic NHL games.

Slaney's inclusion as a legend of Team Canada is in many ways a tribute to the many unlikely or otherwise forgotten names that capture, for a couple of weeks anyway, a nation's attention. Other notable World Junior performances deserving of mention include those of Dale McCourt (1977), Mike Moffat (1982), Gord Kluzak (1982), Jim Sandlak (1986), Jimmy Waite (1987 and 1988), Martin Gendron (1993 and 1994), and Marty Murray (1995).

Opposite page: Slaney celebrates Canada's memorable 1991 world junior title with teammate Felix Potvin. Despite moving on to play professionally, the image of Slaney in a Canadian uniform is his most enduring.

JOHN SLANEY — *St. John's, Newfoundland*

Tournament	GP	G	A	Pts	PIM
1991 World Juniors	7	1	2	3	6
1992 World Juniors	7	1	3	4	0
Team Canada Totals	14	2	5	7	6

Eric Lindros

Above: Lindros celebrates a goal against Czechoslovakia in the 1991 world juniors in Saskatoon. Opposite: Two gold medals with the world junior squads, and action from pre-Olympic play.

NO ACTIVE PLAYER HAS BEEN MORE DEDICATED TO TEAM CANADA than Eric Lindros.

The Big E burst onto the amateur scene as a sixteen-year-old when he was already making headlines as the next great hockey sensation. He was too good to play in the junior leagues, and was already showing an interest in the Canadian national team. In fact he played five games and scored two goals with the Nats while still playing junior B hockey.

At age seventeen Lindros would join the Oshawa Generals of the OHL, but it was the World Junior Championships that gave the whole nation the chance to see their rising star on a grand stage for the first time. He would lead the Canadian national junior team to back-to-back gold medal championships in 1990 and 1991, and an unsuccessful tournament in 1992. In twenty-one career contests at the famous junior championships, Lindros would leave few doubters, with twelve goals, thirty-seven points, and a Top Forward (1991) designation.

Before turning pro, Lindros became the only Canadian player to play in a top-level international tournament without having any National Hockey League experience. The eighteen-year-old phenom was invited to the 1991 Canada Cup training camp and not only made the team but impressed with his physical dominance. The gigantic teenager more than held his own with grizzled NHL warriors, and chipped in with three goals and five points to help Team Canada capture the final Canada Cup championship.

In a perfect world Lindros would have joined the NHL right after that Canada Cup tournament, but he would not see eye to eye with the Quebec Nordiques, who owned his playing rights. He opted to sit out the year and wait for a trade. In the meantime he would return to the Canadian national team with his eyes set on participating in the 1992 Olympic Games.

Lindros would be joined by the likes of Sean Burke, Joe Juneau, and

Jason Woolley, and the team came excruciatingly close to capturing the first Canadian Olympic gold since 1952. Canada would have to settle for silver, however, thanks to a 3-1 defeat by the Russians, then known as the Unified Team, in the final game.

Lindros' NHL situation came to a settlement in the summer of 1992, and the long-awaited phenom turned professional in 1993 with the Philadelphia Flyers. It was an impressive rookie season that was cut short by injuries, and the Flyers didn't make the playoffs that season. Team Canada came calling for Lindros' services and again he eagerly returned to help Canada in the World Championships. Lindros was named the tournament's best forward thanks to his eleven goals and seventeen points in just eight games, although it was not enough to earn Canada a medal.

Injuries would plague Lindros throughout his NHL career, but that would not prevent him from helping Team Canada when he had the opportunity. He represented Canada in the 1996 World Cup of Hockey, which was essentially the Canada Cup with a new name and trophy.

Later, when the Olympics were opened up to NHLers, he readily accepted invites back to the famous tourney. He was captain of the hard luck 1998 Canadian Olympic team that was unfortunate not to get by the eventual gold medal champion Czech Republic.

Lindros managed to recuperate from serious concussion injuries in time to return to the Olympics in 2002. This time Lindros played a quiet and underappreciated role, as Canada captured their first gold medal in exactly fifty years.

Because of his controversial stands against the NHL establishment and serious injuries that have prevented him from becoming as dominant a player as he likely would have been, Lindros has had his fair share of critics over the years. But one area where no one can criticize him is his undying devotion and contributions to Team Canada.

ERIC LINDROS — *London, Ontario*

Tournament	GP	G	A	Pts	PIM
1988-89 National Team	2	1	0	1	0
1989-90 National Team	3	1	0	1	4
1990 World Juniors	7	4	0	4	14
1991 World Juniors	7	6	11	17	6
1991 Canada Cup	8	3	2	5	8
1991-92 National Team	24	19	16	35	34
1992 World Juniors	7	2	8	10	12
1992 Olympic Games	8	5	6	11	5
1993 World Championships	8	11	6	17	10
1996 World Cup of Hockey	8	3	3	6	10
1998 Olympic Games	6	2	3	5	2
2002 Olympic Games	6	1	0	1	8
Team Canada Totals	94	58	55	113	113

Theoren Fleury

FANS OF TEAM CANADA WILL NEVER FORGET the contributions Theoren Fleury has made to Canadian hockey over the years. The NHL superstar represented Canada eight times on the international stage, and was instrumental in Canada's success virtually every time.

International hockey was introduced to Theoren Fleury in 1987 when he was included on the now-infamous world junior squad. The team was en route to capturing a medal, quite possibly the gold, before a bench-clearing brawl broke out between eternal rivals Canada and the Soviet Union. The donnybrook started after an altercation involving Pavel Kostichkin and the feisty Fleury. Both nations were expelled from the tournament because of the "Punch-up in Piestany."

Fleury would return to the world junior stage the following year. Serving as team captain, Fleury put in an all-star performance as he led Canada to a gold medal championship in Moscow. That junior team still holds a special place in the hearts of many Canadians, not just for winning with speed, style, and typical Canadian guts, but also for avenging the embarrassment of the year before.

By the 1990s Fleury had quickly established himself as one of the best hockey players in the world, and Team Canada would be glad he embraced the international game so fully. Following a Stanley Cup championship in his rookie season in 1989, Fleury's Flames would not find much playoff success in the following years. As a result Fleury was available for Team Canada for both the 1990 and 1991 world championships. Fleury scored nine goals and twenty-one points in seventeen games over those two tournaments. His fine play helped Canada capture the silver medal in 1991.

Fleury cemented his status as a top player in the world when the undersized grinder played an important role in the 1991 Canada Cup. Fleury only scored once but put in a memorable performance. Whenever Canada

Fleury readies for a face-off as linemate Wayne Gretzky stands by, during the 1991 Canada Cup. Right: in action with Chris Chelios, and jubilation from the same event.

seemed to need an inspirational moment, Fleury was always able to deliver. Fleury combined his abrasive style with his high skill perfectly in the tournament and was a key member of this undefeated Canada Cup championship team.

Fleury would never miss another top-level international tournament. Team success would not be easily found in the 1996 World Cup of Hockey or the 1998 Olympics but not because of a lack of effort on Fleury's behalf.

Fleury was a surprise inclusion for the 2002 Olympics. Though Fleury was battling personal demons off the ice, team manager Wayne Gretzky never forgot his contributions to Team Canada over the years and included the wily veteran. For long-time Fleury fans it was refreshing to see his game rejuvenated, if only for a short time. Fleury had a spectacular near-goal in the final game that wowed the crowd. Canada would go on to capture their first gold medal in half a century. It was great that this Team Canada legend could be a part of history.

THEOREN FLEURY — *Oxbow, Saskatchewan*

Tournament	GP	G	A	Pts	PIM
1987 World Juniors	6	2	3	5	2
1988 World Juniors	7	6	2	8	4
1990 World Championships	9	4	7	11	10
1991 World Championships	8	5	5	10	8
1991 Canada Cup	7	1	4	5	12
1996 World Cup of Hockey	8	4	2	6	8
1998 Olympics	6	1	3	4	2
2002 Olympics	6	0	2	2	6
Team Canada Totals	57	23	28	51	52

Bill Ranford

BILL RANFORD HAS TO RANK AS ONE OF THE BEST GOALTENDERS IN Team Canada history.

The acrobatic goalie emerged as the best goalie in hockey in the early 1990s, and that was highlighted in the 1991 Canada Cup. With Sean Burke and Eddie Belfour serving as back-ups, Ranford played every minute of every game. With a 1.75 goals against average and a .939 save percentage, Ranford backstopped Canada to the only undefeated Canada Cup championship in tournament history. He was named to the tournament all-star team and the tournament's most valuable player.

Most Canadian goalies at top-level international events seem to have only one chance to star and are often replaced by the time the next big event comes around. But Ranford was able to secure his status as the best goalie in Team Canada history at the world championship level.

Debuting at the world championships in 1993, Ranford was his usual spectacular self when he recorded a 1.86 goals against average and a 5-1 record. Despite the great play in the net, Canada would only be able to finish in fourth place in the overall standings.

Ranford would return in 1994 and was determined to make history. Now a Stanley Cup and Canada Cup champion and MVP, Ranford was never better than in the 1994 World Championships. Allowing just seven goals in six contests, Ranford posted a 1.17 goals against average in the tournament. Those numbers were good enough to earn him a spot on the tournament all-star team — the first Canadian goaltender to do so since Seth Martin did it back in 1966.

More important, Ranford had backstopped Canada to a glorious chance to capture their first world championship banner since Martin's

Trail Smoke Eaters did so in 1961. Ranford held the Canadians in a classic final game against Team Finland that would be decided by a shootout. Ranford was particularly brilliant in the shootout, including on the final shot that captured the first world championship gold medal for Canada in thirty-three long years.

Ranford would have one final showing in a Team Canada jersey, although it was in more of a leadership capacity. The wily veteran was included as the third goalie for Canada's entry at the 1996 World Cup of Hockey. He was the perfect back-up and mentor to Curtis Joseph and Martin Brodeur, but Canada would not be rewarded for their fine play.

An interesting thing happened in his retirement. Disney asked Ranford to do the on-ice goaltending sequences for the 2004 movie *Miracle*. The movie was based on the true story of the 1980 Olympics that saw the mighty Soviets shockingly lose to a bunch of U.S. collegians. Ranford, perhaps the most successful Canadian goalie in international hockey history, was asked to play the role of Jim Craig, the miraculous goalie of 1980 and a legendary figure in USA hockey history. For Ranford, putting on the Team USA jersey was "just bizarre."

As long as his allegiance-switching is confined to the Hollywood big screens, we'll give Bill Ranford the nod as Team Canada's top goalie based on his success and longevity. Honourable mention has to go to Seth Martin and Sean Burke.

Above: A sprawling glove save against Finland in the 1991 Canada Cup in Toronto.
Opposite: Ranford makes a dramatic save during the 1994 World Championships in Milan.
Below: A friendly pat on American forward Pat Lafontaine after stopping him during a 1991 Cup game.

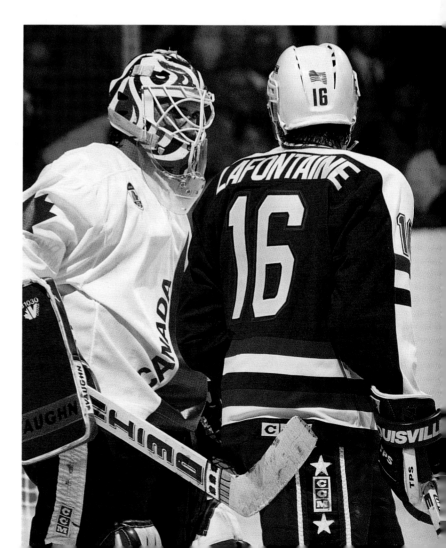

BILL RANFORD — *Brandon, Manitoba*

Tournament	GP	W	L	T	SO	GAA
1991 Canada Cup	8	6	0	2	0	2.00
1993 World Championships	6	5	1	0	2	1.86
1994 World Championships	6	6	0	0	1	1.17
1996 World Cup of Hockey	0	0	0	0	0	0.00
Team Canada Totals	20	17	1	2	3	

Luc Robitaille

Luc Robitaille — *Montreal, Quebec*

Tournament	GP	G	A	Pts	PIM
1986 World Juniors	7	3	5	8	2
1991 Canada Cup	8	1	2	3	10
1994 World Championships	8	4	4	8	2
Team Canada Totals	23	8	11	19	14

LUC ROBITAILLE IS NOT NECESSARILY AN OBVIOUS INCLUSION AS A legend of Team Canada. Despite having a hall-of-fame career that sees him rank as the highest-scoring left winger in National Hockey League history, he has only represented Canada three times.

Robitaille's debut in a Canadian jersey came in 1986 when, in the midst of an incredible junior season, he was named a member of the world junior squad. Overshadowed by the likes of Jim Sandlak, Shayne Corson, and Joe Nieuwendyk, Robitaille quietly chipped in three goals and eight points in seven contests. However the Soviets, led by a young Alexander Semak, proved to be too powerful for Canada in that tournament. Canada would go home with the silver medal.

By 1987 Robitaille had scored forty-five goals in his rookie season and was named the NHL rookie of the year. Somewhat surprisingly, that would not be enough to get him an invite to Team Canada for the 1987 Canada Cup.

But by the next Canada Cup Robitaille was all but a shoo-in for Team Canada. Having taken over Michel Goulet's spot as the best left wing in the game, Robitaille was expected to be a scoring star for Team Canada in the 1991 rendition. Not coach Mike Keenan's stereotypical player, Robitaille suffered in Keenan's system and would only score once and add two assists. But it mattered not, as Canada went undefeated in the entire tournament.

That would be Robitaille's last chance to compete for Canada at the highest level. He was not seriously considered for the 1996 World Cup or the 1998 or 2002 Olympics.

But Robitaille would participate in a Canadian jersey one last time, and it was in that tournament that Robitaille became a Team Canada legend.

With the Los Angeles Kings out of the 1994 NHL playoffs, Robitaille accepted an opportunity to represent Canada at the world championships. Traditionally this tournament has not ranked high in the minds of Canadians. Canada has rarely won the tournament in modern years, since most of Canada's best players are involved in the NHL playoffs. As a result, most of the fans' attention is focused there too. Many Canadian hockey fans dismissed the world championships as unofficial. But in recent years Canadian interest in the tournament has grown, due in part to more Canadian success. That modern success began in 1994, thanks to a memorable goal from Luc Robitaille.

In 1994, many people tuned in as Canada advanced to the gold medal game against Sweden. The game was a classically entertaining game, with the score knotted after regulation and overtime. As a result the game went into a tie-breaking shootout in this rematch of the 1994 Olympic gold medal game. This time Canada would have the last laugh though, as team captain Robitaille scored the game-winning shootout goal to win Canada's first world championship title in thirty-three years. It was the first world championship since the legendary Trail Smoke Eaters represented Canada in 1961.

Not many Canadian players, particularly NHL standouts, are legends of Team Canada based on their performance at the world championships. Six-hundred-plus NHL goal scorer Robitaille breaks that trend by scoring the most significant goal of his career and ending a long Canadian drought at the esteemed tournament.

Above: Robitaille celebrates his winning goal in the shootout to settle the 1994 World Championships in Milan, Canada's first world title since 1961.

Opposite page: Robitaille races Soviet defenders for the puck during the 1991 Canada Cup in Hamilton.

Right: Robitaille's son joins him in the on-ice celebrations.

Martin Brodeur

DESPITE PROVING HIMSELF AS ONE OF THE BEST GOALIES OF HIS ERA, Martin Brodeur always seemed to play second fiddle to his contemporaries in international hockey. That all changed in the 2002 Olympics.

Playing behind Curtis Joseph, Brodeur saw action in just three games in the 1996 world championships. The duo backstopped Canada to a silver medal in Brodeur's international hockey debut.

The pair returned a couple of months later to backstop Canada's entry in the inaugural World Cup of Hockey. Again Brodeur played behind Joseph, and again Canada finished second best.

In 1998, Brodeur was selected for the Canadian Olympic team, thereby following in his father's footsteps. (Denis Brodeur was the starting goalie for Canada's bronze medal–winning entry in the 1956 Olympics in Cortina, Italy.) Unfortunately, Martin Brodeur was not able to play a single minute of Olympic hockey, as he sat on the bench backing up Patrick Roy.

Brodeur returned for the 2002 Olympics in Salt Lake City, and again it looked like he would play back-up. Team Canada coach Pat Quinn selected his NHL goalie Curtis Joseph and it was widely speculated that the Team Canada starting-goalie job was Joseph's to lose. Brodeur was the back-up, with Eddie Belfour serving as the third goalie.

Joseph did end up losing the starting job, and Brodeur was there to save the day. Joseph had a shaky outing in the opening game against Sweden, while Brodeur was solid though unspectacular against Germany. Quinn made the gutsy call of going with Brodeur the rest of the way.

Brodeur seemed to get stronger as the tournament advanced. He was sturdy in a pressure-packed 3-3 tie with the Czech Republic in the final game of the round robin. In the medal round, he led Canada to victories over a tough Finnish team and a surprising Belorussian squad before facing the Americans in the gold medal game. Canada's confidence seemed to be growing with the rise in their goaltender's confidence.

Brodeur saved his best performance for the all-important final, stopping thirty-one shots in a 5-2 Canadian victory. His biggest save came late in the third period. With the score at 3-2 in favour of Canada, Brodeur made a spectacular pad save on a Brett Hull one-timer. Wayne Gretzky called that save "the turning point" of the gold medal game. Certainly the now-classic gold medal story would have been drastically altered if Hull had scored.

Interestingly, Brodeur used a new mask for the Olympic tournament. While most goalies used their familiar NHL mask, Brodeur had a spare mask painted with the Canadian hockey logo just ten days prior to the beginning of the Olympics. The mask also featured the initials of his four children — including an unborn child. On the chin guard were the names of two cities — Salt Lake City and Cortina d'Ampezzo.

Brodeur had another new mask designed for the 2004 World Cup of Hockey, the tournament that would underline his status as the best goalie in the game. He posted a 5-0 record, with one shutout, a 1.00 goals against average, and a .961 save percentage en route to the World Cup title. His defining moment as a true legend of Team Canada came in the semi-final against the Czech Republic. In the must-win game, Brodeur selflessly pulled himself away from the game due to a wrist injury on his catching hand. While many players would have attempted to play with the injury, Brodeur checked his ego at the door and put Team Canada's interests ahead of his own. Brodeur would make a triumphant return in the championship game.

Brodeur has said he keeps his Olympic mask in his trophy room with the gold medal, and undoubtedly his 2004 World Cup mask will soon find a home there too. Given his relatively young age and his new status as Team Canada's favoured incumbent goaltender for future international tournaments, Brodeur will likely make further additions to the mask collection as he battles for more World Cup championships and Olympic gold medals.

MARTIN BRODEUR — *Montreal, Quebec*

Tournament	GP	W	L	T	SO	GAA
1996 World Championships	3	-	-	-	0	3.00
1996 World Cup of Hockey	2	0	1	0	0	4.00
1998 Olympics	0	0	0	0	0	0.00
2002 Olympics	5	4	0	1	0	1.80
2004 World Cup of Hockey	5	5	0	0	1	1.00
Team Canada Totals	15	9	1	1	1	

Opposite: A jubilant Martin Brodeur gestures to the heavens as Canada wins the gold medal in hockey at the 2002 Olympic Games in Salt Lake City.

Right: An NHL pedigree doesn't always guarantee respect, as a Slovakian forward crashes Brodeur's net during the 1996 World Championships.

Scott Niedermayer

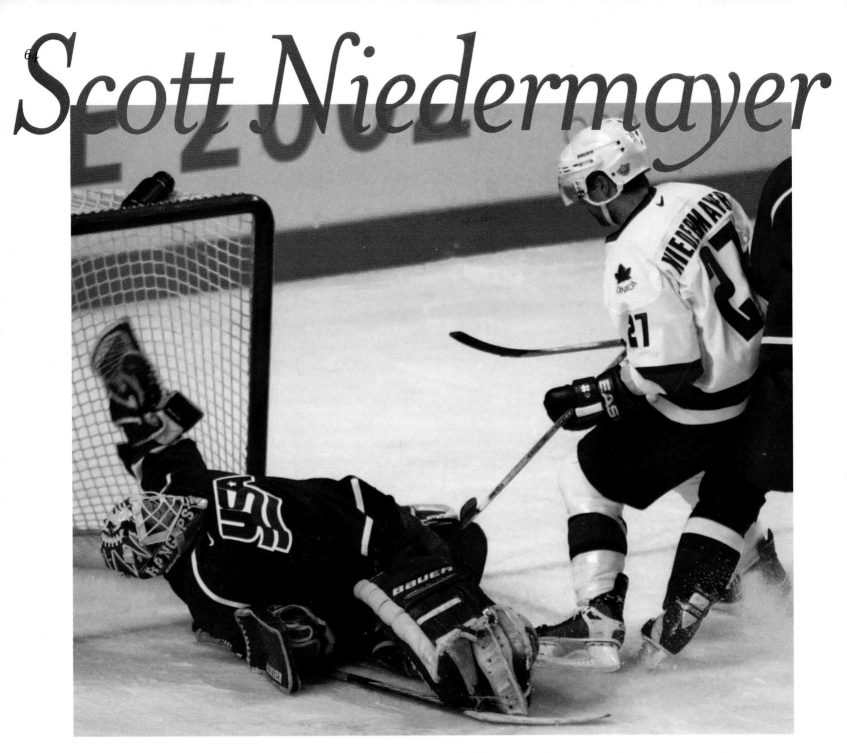

Most Canadian defencemen are developed for the rugged physical game that is employed in the National Hockey League. Though these brutal giants are gems in the NHL, they often have trouble on the larger ice surface of international hockey competition.

That is why Scott Niedermayer has been so important to Team Canada. Simply put, Niedermayer was born to play international hockey. His graceful game is based on skating and passing. His excellent mobility and speed are greatly enhanced on the larger playing area. Though he has turned into more of a defensive stalwart than the offensive juggernaut he was predicted to be, his puck control and passing have made him a top Canadian defenceman.

So respected is Niedermayer's game that Team Canada selected him as one of the first eight players named to the 2002 Olympic squad.

Rob Blake and Chris Pronger joined him as the other obvious choices for Canada's blue line.

Niedermayer's background in international hockey was another factor in his selection for the 2002 Olympic team. He debuted with Team Canada at the World Junior Hockey Championships in 1991, in which he and Eric Lindros guided the team to an impressive gold medal victory. Niedermayer was dominant in the 1992 championships, earning a spot on the post-tournament all-star team despite Canada's weak performance and his own failure to reach the score sheet in seven games. His defensive game on the big ice was already catching the eye of careful observers.

Niedermayer's first international tourney as a professional was the 1996 World Cup of Hockey. He played in all eight games, scoring one goal and four points. With the World Cup being played on traditional NHL-

sized rinks, Canada relied heavily on their rugged behemoths and veterans rather than youthful skilled players like Niedermayer. Perhaps that decision is reflected in Canada's second-place finish in that tournament.

Niedermayer's inclusion in the 2002 Olympics may have seemed obvious, but in 1998 it was not. Despite a strong NHL season that saw him named to the post-season All-Star team, Niedermayer was unthinkably left off the Olympic team. Hindsight is 20-20 of course, but it remains a questionable decision.

The new Team Canada regime, led by Wayne Gretzky, did not make the same mistake. As mentioned earlier, Niedermayer was named one of the "Elite Eight." He scored one goal and one assist in the six Olympic games, but it was his unheralded defensive game that was his true contribution to Canada's first Olympic gold medal in fifty years.

In 2004 Niedermayer jumped at the rare chance to play with his brother Rob at that year's edition of the World Championships. Both were standouts as Team Canada captured back-to-back gold medals on Mother's Day. Scott became only the four-teenth player in hockey history, and only the fourth Canadian, to have earned Olympic, World, and Stanley Cup championship titles in his career. Joe Sakic, Brendan Shanahan, and Rob Blake are the other Canadians to capture this rare hat trick.

In 2004, Niedermayer and Sakic joined Igor Larionov and Viacheslav Fetisov as the only players to capture those three tournaments and the World Cup of Hockey. Fresh off a season that saw him named the NHL's best defenceman, he was thrust into the role of Team Canada's number one rearguard, thanks to injuries to Rob Blake and Chris Pronger. Scott Niedermayer, along with Adam Foote, led a young and inexperi-enced blue line and came away with the World Cup championship, adding yet another international title to his résumé.

SCOTT NIEDERMAYER — *Edmonton, Alberta*

Tournament	GP	G	A	Pts	PIM
1991 World Juniors	7	0	0	0	0
1992 World Juniors	7	0	0	0	10
1996 World Cup of Hockey	8	1	3	4	6
2002 Olympics	6	1	1	2	4
2004 World Championships	9	3	2	5	12
2004 World Cup of Hockey	6	1	1	2	9
Team Canada Totals	43	6	7	13	41

Above: Niedermayer (right) and teammate Brad May show off their medals and champions' plaque after winning the 1991 World Junior title in Saskatoon.

Opposite page: An attack from the back by Niedermayer forces a dramatic save from American goalie Mike Richter during the 2002 Olympic Games at Salt Lake City.

Rob Blake

No one will doubt Rob Blake's status as one of the top defencemen in the National Hockey League over the last decade or so. But somewhat quietly, the Simcoe, Ontario, native has established himself as a key contributor to Team Canada's success, too.

Blake was a rookie defenceman with the Los Angeles Kings during Wayne Gretzky's glory days in the California sun, but the team fell on hard times shortly after an appearance in the 1993 Stanley Cup finals. The lack of NHL playoff success allowed Blake to participate in four World Championships, earning a silver medal in 1991 and two gold medals — one in 1994, the country's first such championship win since 1961, and one in 1997, when he was also named the tournament's best defencemen.

Blake's success on the world stage, coupled with his ascent to stardom in the NHL, made him a lock for competition involving Team Canada at top-level events. Blake was part of the inaugural World Cup of Hockey squad that disappointingly lost to Team USA in 1996. He would only get into four contests, and his hulking presence was noticeably missed when he was out of the lineup.

In 1998, Blake was rightly chosen to be a key part of Team Canada's Olympic plans, as NHL players were allowed full participation for the first time. Though Canada disappointed with a fourth-place finish, Blake was arguably Canada's best player, and was honoured as the best defenceman in the tournament.

Not surprisingly, Blake was one of the initial eight members identified for Canada's 2002 Olympic squad. With his thunderous body checks and booming right-hand shot, Blake was considered by many to be Canada's best defenceman in the tournament once again. Though he wasn't honoured with another best defenceman award, he gladly took the Olympic gold medal home instead.

As long as he remains healthy, Blake has an extraordinary opportunity: He could be the first professional male player to represent Canada at ten top-level tournaments. While Sean Burke, Eric Lindros, and James Patrick currently sit at nine tournaments each, their age makes it unlikely that they will get another shot. Steve Yzerman has participated in eight tournaments, though age and injuries negatively enter his equation too. Injuries cost Blake the opportunity to help Canada capture the 2004 World Cup of Hockey.

Blake's continued devotion, coupled with important contributions and successes on the world stage, already makes him a legend. With better luck on the injury front, no doubt there will be future chapters to write.

Rob Blake — *Simcoe, Ontario*

Tournament	GP	G	A	Pts	PIM
1991 World Championships	2	0	2	2	0
1994 World Championships	8	0	2	2	34
1996 World Cup of Hockey	4	0	1	1	0
1997 World Championships	11	2	2	4	22
1998 Olympic Games	6	1	1	2	2
1998 World Championships	5	1	0	1	6
1999 World Championships	10	2	5	7	12
2002 Olympic Games	6	1	2	3	2
Team Canada Totals	52	7	15	22	78

Above: Some rough treatment along the boards from Belarus at the 2002 Olympic Games in Salt Lake City.
Opposite page: Blake moves in to cover a rebound from Martin Brodeur's acrobatic save during the same event.

Joe Sakic

Joe Sakic — *Burnaby, BC*

Tournament	GP	G	A	Pts	PIM
1986-87 National Team	1	0	0	0	0
1988 World Juniors	7	3	1	4	2
1991 World Championships	10	6	5	11	0
1994 World Championships	8	4	3	7	0
1996 World Cup of Hockey	8	2	2	4	6
1998 Olympic Games	4	1	2	3	4
2002 Olympic Games	6	4	3	7	0
2004 World Cup of Hockey	6	4	2	6	2
Team Canada Totals	50	24	18	42	14

Right: Sakic's scoring touch produced two goals against the USA en route to a 5-2 gold-medal victory at Salt Lake City.

Opposite page: Sakic had a big year in 1991, helping Canada to a silver medal at the World Championships. Here, he's shown in Canada Cup preliminaries. He was a late cut from that roster.

Joe Sakic's career contributions to Team Canada have been largely overlooked. The 1988 World Junior gold medallist twice represented Canada at the World Championships early in his career. Those were tough days for a young Sakic, as his Quebec Nordiques were struggling terribly in the NHL. But in 1991 and 1994 Sakic was able to overcome professional disappointment to play for his country.

Sakic would not find disappointment on the international stage. In 1991, his six goals and eleven points in ten games led Canada to a silver medal. In 1994, Sakic was part of Canada's first world champion team in over three decades when he helped Canada defeat Finland in a thrilling shootout victory.

In 1995, the fortunes of Sakic's Nordiques/Colorado Avalanche quickly rose, leaving Sakic unavailable for Team Canada duty at the world championships. But he would be able to step up to the highest level of international hockey in 1996. That year, the Canada Cup tournament was re-incarnated as the World Cup of Hockey. Sakic played well but not great in the tournament, scoring two goals and four points in eight contests. Canada would run into a brick wall in the form of USA goalie Mike Richter and lose the championship despite dominating most of the games.

Canada and Sakic would get a chance to redeem themselves in 1998, when the Olympic Games welcomed all NHL competitors for the first time. However, all did not go well for Canada or Sakic. Canada ran into another hot goaltender, this time Dominik Hasek of the Czech Republic. Sakic, a gifted scorer who likely would have been involved in the famous tie-breaking shootout against the Czechs, had to sit out the game and the following bronze medal match after straining a ligament in his left knee in a game against Kazakhstan.

All of these international disappointments were quickly forgotten come 2002. Sakic returned to the Olympic Games and as much as anybody on the team led the nation to its first Olympic gold medal championship in half a century. Sakic led all Canadian scorers with four goals and seven points, including two goals and two assists in the gold medal game against the United States. Sakic's single-game performance was arguably the most memorable in Canadian history. His four-point outburst garnered him the unofficial Most Valuable Player award from the media.

The competition also acknowledged Sakic as making the difference between gold and silver.

"They won [the gold] as a team, but sometimes it takes one individual," said American defenceman Chris Chelios. "Joe Sakic really stepped it up. There are guys on both teams that know what it takes to win, and he had a heck of a game right from the start."

For Sakic it was a season to remember. Just a few months earlier he had led his Avalanche to the Stanley Cup as well as winning the NHL's Hart, Pearson, and Byng trophies. He had clearly established himself as the best player in the world at the turn of the century.

"He's a great player, who has great hands," said USA goalie Mike Richter, voted the 2002 Olympics' best goaltender. "All their players were playing well and skating hard, but Joe just seems to know where to go to get in scoring position. Even if he is not in scoring position, he has a great sense of the net, so you have to honour him."

Sakic proved his greatness once again at the 2004 World Cup of Hockey. Centring Canada's top line with dream linemates Jarome Iginla and Mario Lemieux, Sakic led the way with four goals. His six points put him second highest on the team. He excelled defensively as well, particularly in the face-off circle. The line probably should have had triple its statistics but all three were snake-bitten early in the tournament. Regardless, Sakic may have been Canada's most consistent performer at the World Cup.

Paul Kariya

PAUL KARIYA — *Vancouver, British Columbia*

Tournament	GP	G	A	Pts	PIM
1992 World Juniors	6	1	1	2	2
1993 World Juniors	7	2	6	8	2
1993 World Championships	8	2	7	9	0
1993-94 National Team	23	7	34	41	2
1994 Olympic Games	8	3	4	7	2
1994 World Championships	8	5	7	12	2
1996 World Championships	8	4	3	7	2
2002 Olympic Games	6	3	1	4	0
Team Canada Totals	74	27	63	90	12

Kariya has made tremendous contributions to Team Canada over the years. With the larger ice surfaces in Europe, his outstanding skating skills make him an even greater threat to opponents.

ASIDE FROM ERIC LINDROS, NO ACTIVE NHL PLAYER HAS BEEN MORE dedicated to Team Canada than Paul Kariya. Unfortunately for Kariya, injuries have not always allowed him to play in the biggest of tournaments.

Kariya first rose to international prominence in back-to-back World Junior performances. His speed and puck skills were magnified on the big ice. The little left-winger's style was perfectly designed for international hockey, and he quickly embraced it. With two goals and a team-leading six assists, he was a major contributor to Canada's gold medal junior championship in 1993. He was also named to the tournament all-star team.

Kariya, who was a standout athlete and student at the University of Maine, got a rare invite as an undrafted junior player to the national team for the '93 World Championships. Despite his youth, Kariya never looked out of place, scoring two goals and nine points in eight games. However, Canada failed to capture a medal.

Kariya's experience with the two international tournaments inspired an alternate career path. Unable to reach a contract after being drafted by Anaheim, Kariya dropped out of school in order to pursue an Olympic dream that at that time was not open to most NHL players. Kariya took full advantage of what he thought might be his only opportunity to realize his childhood dream of participating in the Olympic Games.

Kariya played twenty-three games with the national team that season in preparation for the Olympics, and scored an amazing thirty-four assists and forty-one points. At the Olympics, he led Team Canada in scoring with seven points in eight games, but Canada fell painfully short of the gold medal. The final game went into the dreaded shootout. The two teams remained tied after the first round of penalty shots, including a Kariya tally. But in the subsequent sudden death round, Kariya failed to match Sweden's Peter Forsberg's goal. The result was a 3-2 loss. Canada would have to find consolation in the silver medal.

Later that season, Kariya redeemed himself. The popular winger led

Canada with five goals and twelve points as Team Canada defeated Finland for the world championship. That game too went into the shootout, with Canada tasting victory for a rare turn. Kariya was named the tournament's best forward.

Kariya made the jump to the NHL the following season, but returned to the world championships in 1996. Once again he was named the tournament's best forward as Canada captured the silver medal.

By this time, Kariya was undoubtedly one of the best players in the NHL and the world. He was going to be counted on heavily as professionals dominated top-level international competition and the Canada Cup was reborn as the World Cup. Kariya was an obvious inclusion on the team, but would have to miss the entire tournament with an abdominal injury.

A similar story played out in 1998. For the first time, the NHL allowed its best to play in the Olympic Games. The Olympics meant more to Kariya than to most players, especially since these Olympics were held in Japan where Kariya's family originated. However, Kariya would have another devastating setback. Despite being selected to play once again, he missed the entire tournament due to a serious concussion suffered about a month before the Olympics began. Looking to make up for the silver medal in 1994, Kariya had made the 1998 Olympics a huge goal. It turned out to be "the biggest disappointment" of his career.

Kariya was finally able to represent his country as a top-level NHL player in 2002. With the Olympics in Salt Lake City, Utah, Kariya was one of the initial eight players named to the team, and this time remained healthy through to the tournament. Often playing with the incomparable Mario Lemieux, Kariya scored three goals and four points in six Olympic games as Team Canada captured its first gold medal in half a century.

For the NHL superstar who as a kid dreamed of winning Olympic gold, this will undoubtedly rank as one of Paul Kariya's greatest moments.

Steve Yzerman

STEVE YZERMAN MIGHT BE THE ULTIMATE CANADIAN HOCKEY HERO. He complements his incredible hockey skills with such stereotypical Canadian traits as grit, heart, and determination.

Yzerman first donned the Canadian maple leaf jersey during the 1983 World Junior Championships held in Leningrad. Yzerman, just seventeen years of age, scored five points in seven games, despite playing second fiddle to highly touted Mario Lemieux. Canada would win the bronze medal.

Yzerman made gigantic career leaps the next season. Not only did he jump directly into the NHL, but he earned a Team Canada spot after attending the 1984 Canada Cup training camp. Just three months past his nineteenth birthday, it was an impressive feat by the young Yzerman to earn a spot on a roster that also sported the likes of Wayne Gretzky, Mark Messier, Peter Stastny, and Brent Sutter at centre ice. Yzerman, Canada's youngest player, saw only limited ice time in four contests, but he took the opportunity to learn from Canada's best.

With Yzerman's quick rise to the NHL's elite, it was widely expected that he would be a key contributor to Canada in future international tournaments. However, disappointment would haunt "Stevie Wonder" during both the 1987 and 1991 Canada Cup tournaments. On both occasions coach Mike Keenan snubbed him. In 1987 he came off a ninety-point season in the NHL but was cut by Keenan in training camp. Keenan clearly favoured the muckers and grinders. Then in 1991 Yzerman made the team but was scratched in the initial two games and never got a chance to play. Each team was only allowed to use twenty skaters, and since Keenan was forced to save the last roster spot for a defenceman in case of injuries, Yzerman became the odd man out, despite having a 108-point season. It is needless to say that Yzerman was greatly hurt by all this, but he showed his usual professional attitude and Canadian pride when he had the opportunity.

NHL playoff success was not easy to come by for Yzerman's Detroit Red Wings in the 1980s. As a result Yzerman had three opportunities to represent Canada at the world championships. He was simply outstanding in 1985 and even more so in 1989 and 1990 when he helped Canada capture two silver medals. His eighteen goals and twenty-one assists for thirty-nine points in twenty-one world championship games ranks him as one of the all-time Canadian greats in the spring tournament.

Despite his success at the world championships, Yzerman still desired to represent Canada at a top-level international event. He eagerly accepted an invitation to join Team Canada for the World Cup of Hockey in 1996. Canada dominated the reincarnated Canada Cup tournament, but ran into a red-hot goalie named Mike Richter of Team USA. Richter would impressively steal victory away from the Canadians, but it was not for a lack of effort on Yzerman's part. He had a team-best plus-four rating while scoring two goals and three points. Both of his goals in the tournament were game winners,

including the overtime game winner in Game One of the finals against the Americans.

Yzerman would have to taste more bitterness in his pursuit to return Canada to the top of the hockey world. In Nagano in 1998, Canada was playing well before running into nemesis Dominik Hasek and the Czech Republic in the semi-finals. The Czechs smothered Team Canada in regulation and in overtime. The game remained tied and went to the dreaded tie-breaking shootout format. With Yzerman and Gretzky sitting on the bench, Hasek shut out the Canadian shooters, while Robert Reichel was able to score. The nation's gold medal hopes were also blanked.

There is no doubt that Yzerman's sweetest moment in a Canadian jersey came at the 2002 Olympics held in Salt Lake City. The thirty-six-year-old showed tremendous leadership and grit, playing on a badly hobbled knee that would have kept most players off the ice. Yzerman played incredibly, finishing tied with Mario Lemieux for second in team scoring while inspiring his teammates on to victory. In the gold medal game Yzerman and linemate Joe Sakic were the dominant force, though his knee still bothered him greatly. In fact, after a strong opening period, Yzerman had to sit out the entire second period because of the injury. He returned in the third period and set up Jarome Iginla's 4-2 goal to all but officially clinch the championship.

In fifty-seven games for Team Canada, spanning over almost twenty years, he scored twenty-five goals and added thirty assists for fifty-five points. Steve Yzerman is a true legend of Canadian hockey.

In terms of his scoring abilities, Yzerman was at the height of his career when he joined the national team roster for the 1991 Canada Cup. Below, he's shown at practice and at right, in action as captain during a pre-tournament game against the USA in Montreal.

STEVE YZERMAN — *Cranbrook, British Columbia*

Tournament	GP	G	A	Pts	PIM
1983 World Juniors	7	2	3	5	2
1984 Canada Cup	4	0	0	0	0
1985 World Championships	10	3	4	7	6
1989 World Championships	8	5	7	12	2
1990 World Championships	10	10	10	20	8
1996 World Cup of Hockey	6	2	1	3	0
1998 Olympics	6	1	1	2	10
2002 Olympics	6	2	4	6	2
Team Canada Totals	57	25	30	55	30

Ryan Smyth

One of the gutsiest and grittiest players ever to join Team Canada, Ryan Smyth's willingness to battle for every puck epitomizes Canadian hockey pride.

Above: battling Finland at the 2004 World Championships.

Right: Dishing a hit on USA's Brian Leetch at the 2002 Olympics.

Opposite: As captain for Team Canada, Ryan Smyth poses in Helsinki's Hartwell Arena with the 2003 IIHF world championship trophy, moments after Anson Carter's remarkable overtime wraparound goal gave Canada a memorable 3-2 win over Sweden.

RYAN SMYTH WOULD NEVER TURN DOWN AN INVITATION to play for Team Canada, but he'd probably enjoy not being invited one of these years.

Smyth is something of an oddity in modern-day hockey — he has participated in six consecutive world hockey championships, setting a record for games played by a Canadian NHLer at the Worlds in the process. Such frequent participation in the tournament is extremely rare in modern times, since most of the world's best players are busy in the Stanley Cup playoffs when the Worlds are scheduled. The national teams at the World Championships are made up of players from NHL teams who either did not qualify for the playoffs or were knocked out early in the first round.

And that is where the disappointment lies for Smyth. Though he relishes the opportunity to play for his nation, his Edmonton Oilers have not had much luck in the post-season. The only way Smyth would not play for Team Canada at future World Championships is if the Oilers ever get that long playoff run that has eluded them in recent years.

Smyth may lack the innate talents of some other players, but he provides leadership and inspiration through his determined vigour and nose for the net. Those traits make him an obvious choice not only for Team Canada but also for captain. Smyth played that role in the 2001, 2002, 2003, and 2004 world tournaments, capturing back-to-back gold medals in the last two years.

"It's a huge honour not only to play for your country but to be asked so many times to come over," Smyth said. "I love this game and [Team Canada] have been so great to me over the years."

Smyth's dedication to Team Canada was not forgotten when Hockey Canada was selecting the 2002 Olympic team. Despite suffering through a serious ankle injury in the weeks prior to the Olympics, Smyth played on a physical line, often paired with Owen Nolan, Michael Peca, or Eric Lindros. He scored just one assist in six games but was a significant contributor to Canada's first Olympic gold medal win in half a century.

Smyth was also a major contributor to the 2004 World Cup of Hockey title. Playing on a line with Vincent Lecavalier and Dany Heatley, Smyth scored three goals. Interestingly enough, though he is the most senior of all players in terms of times representing Canada, this tournament marked the first time Smyth was able to wear the red maple leaf in Canada. All of his Team Canada experience has come overseas or while in the USA.

Though Canadian hockey fans enjoy having Ryan Smyth representing the nation at the annual world hockey championships, we all hope that one of these years we will not be able to ask him to come back yet again.

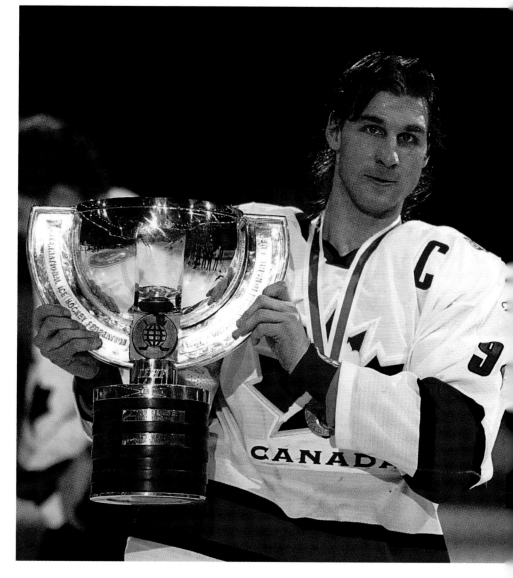

RYAN SMYTH — *Banff, Alberta*

Tournament	GP	G	A	Pts	PIM
1995 World Juniors	7	2	5	7	4
1999 World Championships	10	0	2	2	12
2000 World Championships	9	3	6	9	0
2001 World Championships	7	2	3	5	4
2002 Olympics	6	0	1	1	0
2002 World Championships	7	4	0	4	2
2003 World Championships	9	2	2	4	2
2004 World Championships	9	2	2	4	2
2004 World Cup of Hockey	6	3	1	4	2
Team Canada Totals	70	18	22	40	28

Vincent Lecavalier

EVERY GREAT CANADIAN VICTORY FEATURES A SIGNATURE MOMENT. More often than not, the moment is a dramatic winning goal. The goal goes on to become a part of Canadian folklore, as young boys and girls grow up dreaming of scoring the famous goal and becoming a legend of Team Canada.

In 1972, Paul Henderson scored "the goal heard around the world," clinching the Summit Series victory with just twenty-six seconds left to play in the series. By doing so he defined Canadian hockey heroics. For most Canadians, it will always be that Summit Series winning goal that stands as the greatest goal of all time.

In the 1987 Canada Cup, two of hockey's all-time greats dared to equal the heroics and the dramatics. Mario Lemieux took a soft drop pass from Wayne Gretzky to defeat the Soviets with just 1:26 left in an exhausting three-game Canada Cup final.

There are other great moments: In 1976 it was Darryl Sittler's overtime marker against Vladimir Dzurilla. In 1984 Mike Bossy's deflection upset the favoured Soviets. In 1991 Steve Larmer's breakaway goal clinched an undefeated Canada Cup championship. In 2002 Joe Sakic and Jayna Hefford scored the dramatic goals to earn Canadian Olympic gold medals.

And in the 2004 World Cup of Hockey, it was Vincent Lecavalier who provided the memorable moment.

Canada was in a tough semi-final showdown with the Czech Republic. The Czechs employed a heavy forecheck, and really had Canada on the ropes much of the game. Canada was perhaps lucky not to lose, as they were under particularly heavy pressure early in the first overtime period. That's when Lecavalier showed his magic.

Lecavalier broke into the Czech zone alone and swooped behind the net. He centred the puck, and got it back all alone in front of Czech goalie Tomas Vokoun. Though he had trouble corralling the puck at first, he used his great patience and skill to roof the puck over a sprawled Vokoun from a very bad angle.

"I missed my first shot and I knew I didn't have much time," said Lecavalier. "I just turned around and shot as quickly as I could. With the angle I had, I got pretty lucky. Scoring for your country in overtime — that's pretty high in my career."

The entire tournament was a high in Lecavalier's career. Lecavalier is generally considered to be the most skilled young player in the game, though he has yet to develop his game to his fullest potential. That

was the main reason Lecavalier was initially omitted from the Team Canada roster, even though he had an incredible 2004 NHL playoff that was capped with a Stanley Cup victory.

Lecavalier was later added to the Canadian team to replace the injured Steve Yzerman. While Yzerman is a Team Canada legend in his own right and can never be replaced, Lecavalier was the perfect choice. No player showed as much creativity as he did, and he was as physical as any other player. He ended up leading Team Canada in scoring with seven points, and was only one point off the tournament scoring lead. For his incredible tournament, he was named the World Cup of Hockey 2004's Most Valuable Player. He was also named to the tournament all-star team.

The legend of Vincent Lecavalier has only just begun. He will return to lead Canada into future battles.

VINCENT LECAVALIER — *Montreal, Quebec*

Tournament	GP	G	A	Pts	PIM
1998 World Juniors	7	1	1	2	4
2001 World Championships	7	3	2	5	29
2004 World Cup of Hockey	7	2	5	7	8
Team Canada Totals	21	6	8	14	41

Opposite page: Lecavalier moves to corral a rebound and score the overtime winning goal against the Czech Republic in the 2004 World Cup.

Left: Lecavalier in action for Canada's world junior team.

Before There Was a Team Canada

THE TERM "TEAM CANADA" DID NOT REALLY EXIST PRIOR TO THE 1972 Summit Series, but international hockey involving some great Canadian teams and players certainly did.

Up until the 1960s, Canada sent its amateur champions, winners of the Allan Cup, to compete against the best in the world in such tournaments as the Olympics and the world championships. They competed under the name "Canada," though within Canada they were still often referred to by their club team name.

Sending the Allan Cup champions to represent Canada internationally proved to be good enough until the 1950s, as Canada won nearly every tournament available. However, in the 1950s and '60s the Soviets and Czechoslovakians had developed their game to the point where they were too strong for Canadian amateurs. Canada realized it would have to take a different tack to compete on the world hockey stage, and in 1964 developed a national team.

Though the earlier teams did not bear the Team Canada moniker, the contributions of the players to our nation's hockey heritage cannot be ignored. Here's a look at some of Canada's long-ago amateur heroes of international hockey.

Frank Fredrickson

The Winnipeg Falcons represented Canada at the very first Olympic hockey competition, which was held as a demonstration sport at the Antwerp Summer Games of 1920. Fredrickson, who ranks as one of the game's early greats, undoubtedly led the Falcons. He had twelve goals in three games as Canada outscored the opposition 29-1. Fredrickson went on to score seven of Canada's twelve goals in the gold medal game against Sweden.

Harry Watson

The Toronto Granites represented Canada in the 1924 Olympics, and they proved to be far too much for the competition. They easily won the gold medal, outscoring their opponents 110-3. Harry Watson was the scoring star for the Granites, notching an amazing thirty-six goals in just five games (no assists were recorded in this tournament). He scored hat tricks in every game, including eleven goals in a 30-0 victory over Czechoslovakia. Two nights later he scored thirteen times in a 33-0 victory over Switzerland. Needless to say, Watson holds all goal-scoring records in Olympic competition.

Reginald "Hooley" Smith

Before embarking upon a Hall of Fame NHL career, Reginald "Hooley" Smith first teamed with Harry Watson and Bert McCaffery to guide the Toronto Granites to the 1924 Olympic gold medal. Smith scored eighteen goals in five games. In four of those five games he scored at least four goals. Smith joins Watson, Fredrickson, Harry Sinden, Wayne Gretzky, Ray Bourque, and Mario Lemieux as the only Canadian Olympians to be enshrined in the Hockey Hall of Fame, although a few more names will be added to that list soon.

The Winnipeg Falcons team seen here in 1920, from left to right are: G. Sigurjonson, H. Axford, W. Byron, S. Halderson, F. Fredrickson, W.A. Hewitt, K. Johanesson, M. Goodman, A. Woodman, B. Benson, F.Fridfinnson, and W.Fridfinnson.

Dave Trottier

Speedy Dave Trottier (no relation to Bryan Trottier) entered the NHL with much fanfare back in 1928. The Montreal Maroons offered him the princely sum of $10,000 to turn professional. Trottier was a much-heralded amateur with the University of Toronto Varsity Graduates. In 1928 the Grads represented Canada at the Olympic Games. It was in St. Moritz, Switzerland, that Trottier cemented his amateur celebrity status with twelve goals in just three games.

Victor Lindquist

This Winnipeg right winger captured two gold medals. In 1932 he and Walter Monson led Canada to the championship at the Lake Placid Olympics, amidst the first hint of a Canadian-American hockey rivalry. In 1935 he returned to the world stage, representing Canada at the world championships in Davos, Switzerland. Lindquist later served as an official for three decades, and is a member of the International Ice Hockey Hall of Fame.

Murray Dowey

The Royal Canadian Air Force (RCAF) Flyers, coached by the legendary Frank Boucher, represented Canada in the 1948 Olympics in Switzerland. Canada faced some high-scoring competition from the Czechoslovakians and Americans, but captured another gold medal thanks to the great goaltending of Aircraftsman 2 Murray Dowey. Dowey allowed only five goals in eight games and backstopped Canada to a 7-0-1 record. Dowey posted five shutouts in those Olympics; no other Canadian goalie has ever posted more than two in their entire Olympic career. Dowey's showing has to rank as one of Canada's greatest international goaltending performances.

The Warwick Brothers

In 1955 the rollicking Warwick Brothers — Grant, Bill, and Dick — became the toast of Canada. The previous year saw the Soviets capture their first world championship by destroying the Toronto East York Lyndhursts 7-2. In 1955, the Warwicks led the Penticton Vees to a 5-0 victory over the defending champions. The Vees and the Warwicks received much fanfare from the convincing victory. Grant was probably the best player of the three, but also served as head coach and chose to concentrate strictly on coaching in the historic game.

Jean-Paul Lamirande

After making several stops in the NHL and AHL, Jean-Paul Lamirande became a top senior hockey player in Canada. Twice he represented Canada at the world championships. In 1958 he was an addition to the Allan Cup champion Whitby Dunlops, and in 1959 his Belleville McFarlands earned the right to travel overseas. Both times he won gold, and in 1959 he was named the best defenceman in the entire tournament.

Harry Sinden

Sinden is best known internationally as the coach of Team Canada in the 1972 Summit Series. But it was his background in international hockey that made him the obvious choice to coach the NHL stars. Sinden captained the Whitby Dunlops to the 1958 world championship, thanks to seven straight wins. Sinden returned for the Olympic Winter Games in 1960 in Squaw Valley, winning the silver medal.

Jackie McLeod

McLeod devoted several years to Canada's international hockey efforts. In 1961 he was a key member of the Trail Smoke Eaters. He scored ten goals and fourteen points in seven games as Canada won their last

world championship gold until the 1990s. He returned to Europe in 1962 with the Galt Terriers and in 1963 again with the Smoke Eaters. He later turned to coaching Canada's national team and guided the team to the bronze medal in the 1968 Olympics.

Pictured here on Feb. 3, 1955, wearing their Canada uniforms for the first time are the Penticton Vees hockey team who represented Canada at the World Hockey Championships in Germany in 1955. The Vees, in taking the Allan Cup in 1955, ensured their trip to the U.S.S.R. Seen here from L to R are: Front Row, Mike Shabaga, Bill Warwick, Ivan McLelland, Don Moog, Dick Warwick, Jack McIntyre. 2nd Row: Ed Kassian, Bernie Bathgate, Don Berry, Grant Warwick, Jim Fairburn, George McAvoy, Dino Mascotto. Back Row: Harry Harris, Hal Tarala, Kev Conway, Jack McDonald, Doug Kilburn, Ernie Rucks.

Connie Broden

Connie Broden's unique feat in 1958 earns him mention as a legendary figure in Team Canada history. At the time, Broden was a spare piece of the dynastic puzzle put together by the Montreal Canadiens. When the Whitby Dunlops had earned the right to represent Canada in the world championships, they asked the Montreal Canadiens if they could borrow Ralph Backstrom to bolster Canada's chances. Montreal refused, but offered Connie Broden. Broden scored at least one goal in every game played in that tournament, totalling twelve goals and nineteen points in just seven games, leading Canada to the gold medal. Upon his return to Montreal, he then helped the Canadiens win the Stanley Cup. Broden became the first player in hockey history to win a world championship and Stanley Cup championship in the same year.

Adolphe "Addy" Tambellini

Adolphe "Addy" Tambellini was a member of the famous Trail Smoke Eaters team that won world championship gold in 1961, the last Canadian championship until the 1990s. He returned in 1963, and though the team would only finish fourth overall, the speedy Tambellini was named to the tournament all-star team. Tambellini made one more appearance in 1967 as a member of the four-year-old Canadian national team, helping the team win bronze. Tambellini's son Steve later became a NHL regular and a significant contributor to Canadian international appearances as a player and administrator. In 2004 Tambellini's grandson Jeff represented Canada at the world junior championships, making the Tambellinis the first family to have three-generation represent Canada in international hockey

Father Bauer's

FATHER DAVE BAUER BECAME A LEGEND OF CANADIAN INTERNATIONAL hockey when he created the first national hockey team to represent Canada internationally in such tournaments as the world championships and the Olympics.

At the time, the world championships and Olympics were open only to amateur players. Since virtually every top Canadian player was a professional in the National Hockey League, Canada never could send their best players to such tournaments. As described earlier, usually top senior teams would represent Canada. Up until 1954 these teams were able to easily defeat most opponents they faced in international competition. However, things would forever change in 1954 when the Soviet Union, stocked with players whose amateur status was questionable in the eyes of many, entered the world championships for the first time. Within a few short years the Soviets and soon the Czechoslovakians became the ultimate teams on the international stage. Canada's senior teams were no longer able to grab the glory from them.

In order to recapture success on the international stage, Bauer, brother of former NHL standout Bobby Bauer, proposed an amateur alternative. Players would play the season for the national team. In lieu of payment, they were given room and board, as well as tuition to University of British Columbia in Vancouver, where they were originally based. In order to retain their amateur status, the players could not draw a salary from the team, but the offer of a free education appealed to several players.

The Canadian national team, better known as the "Nats," had a short life. It lasted only from 1964 through 1970, when the Canadian governing hockey bodies boycotted all International Ice Hockey Federation (IIHF) events until Canada, like the U.S.S.R., was allowed to use its best players. The Nats collected bronze medals in the 1966 and 1967 World Championships and 1968 Olympics, and had a small but dedicated following of supporters.

Here's a look at some of the legends of the "Nats."

While never widely known in his own country, Martin was something of a hero to European goaltenders, including a young Vladislav Tretiak.

Seth Martin

Although many Canadian fans won't recognize his name, perhaps the best Canadian goaltender in international hockey was Seth Martin. While never widely known in his own country, Martin was something of a hero to European goaltenders, including a young Vladislav Tretiak.

Martin first played on the international scene as a member of the Trail Smoke Eaters. The Smoke Eaters had won the 1961 Allan Cup as Canada's amateur senior champions. At that time Canada was still sending its senior champions to the IIHF's world championships. The Smoke Eaters would be the last Canadian amateur team to win the world championship. Martin was spectacular, allowing only six goals in five games, and was named the tournament's top goalie.

Martin and the Smoke Eaters returned to the Worlds in 1963. Martin again was named the top goaltender, although Canada would finish in fourth place.

The following year Canada developed its first national team program to represent the nation at international hockey events. Martin was quickly recruited for the team. He jumped at the chance and was able to represent Canada in the 1964 Olympics. He would return home to Trail following the Olympics, but was welcomed back to represent Canada in the 1966 and 1967 World Championships.

Martin would turn professional with the NHL's St. Louis Blues in 1967–68 but would return to amateur status after just one season.

Goaltending had always been a weak area of the European game. Martin's spectacular play in these international events makes him a Canadian legend. However, he is more of a Canadian legend in Europe than he ever was in his own country.

"The Europeans think of Seth Martin as much as we think of Vladislav Tretiak here in Canada," says hockey researcher Ron Boileau.

"Nats"

Terry O'Malley

One of the original members of Father Bauer's national team, O'Malley was one of the first Canadians to dedicate his career almost entirely to the international game. He was with the Nats from 1963 through to the program's dismantling in 1970. The one-time Nats team captain competed in three world championships (1965, 1966, and 1969) as well as three Olympic Games (1964, 1968, and a surprise return in 1980 as a thirty-nine-year-old), earning one bronze medal (1968).

O'Malley, a member of the IIHF Hall of Fame, spent most of the 1970s playing and coaching teams in Japan.

Marshall Johnston

Perhaps better known to modern fans as the former general manager of the Ottawa Senators, Marshall Johnston was once a dedicated international hockey player. Johnston would earn bronze medals in the 1966 and 1967 World Championships and the 1968 Olympics. He also participated in the 1964 Olympics.

Johnston would move on to enjoy regular NHL employment through to his retirement in 1974. He then returned to the international game as a coach. He acted as an assistant coach at the 1978 IIHF World Championship and was named head coach for both the 1979 and 1982 tournaments.

Roger Bourbonnais

Roger Bourbonnais was a junior standout that opted for Father Bauer's national team program rather than turn to the world of professional hockey. Bourbonnais was one of the few offensive threats on the generally defence-oriented team. He played with the Nats from the time of its inception in 1963–64 until the team withdrew from international competition in 1970.

In his time, Bourbonnais played in two Olympic Winter Games and four world championships. His trophy case includes a bronze medal from the Grenoble Olympics in 1968, as well as bronze medals for the 1964, 1966, and 1967 World Championships. He was later inducted into the IIHF Hall of Fame.

Bourbonnais never turned professional, as the highly intelligent academic pursued a successful law career instead.

Fran Huck

A junior standout, Fran Huck joined Father Bauer's Nats in 1965–66. He would be an offensive threat on the team until its disbandment in 1970. He led all Canadian scorers in scoring during bronze medal performances in the 1966 and 1967 World Championships and the 1968 Olympics.

Huck would go on to a successful professional career, mostly in the World Hockey Association.

Morris Mott

Over the years it is likely that many students at Brandon University in Manitoba were quite surprised to discover that their history professor was a former NHL player. Morris Mott played three unnoticeable seasons with the California Golden Seals from 1972 through 1975.

But if his students were to look further into his hockey history, they'd see Professor Mott was a legendary contributor to Canada in the later 1960s as well.

Mott was another regular on the Nats, joining the team in 1965. He earned bronze medals in the 1966 and 1967 Worlds and the 1968 Olympics. In those Olympics he led all Canadian players, with five goals scored, including four in one game. Mott would return for the 1969 World Championships.

After his NHL career was over he returned to the international game and played in Sweden in 1975–76 for his last full season of hockey.

Barry MacKenzie

Barry MacKenzie was a disciple of Father Bauer dating back to their junior hockey days. Instead of attempting a professional career, MacKenzie joined Canada's National Team in the 1963–64 season. He represented his country at the 1964 Olympic Winter Games in Innsbruck, finishing just out of the medals in fourth place. MacKenzie also represented Canada at the 1965, 1966, and 1967 IIHF World Championships, winning the bronze medal in both the 1966 and 1967 tournaments. MacKenzie returned for one final season with the Nats, capturing the 1968 Olympic bronze medal. The following season MacKenzie, a close friend of Team Canada legend Terry O'Malley, finally turned pro and played briefly for the Minnesota North Stars.

National Team

THE ORIGINAL CANADIAN NATIONAL TEAM PROGRAM DEPARTED FROM the international hockey scene at the beginning of the 1970s in a dispute with the IIHF over the use of professional players in international events. The dispute lasted seven seasons, ending only when professional players were allowed to represent Canada, although few of the top NHL players actually would play due to NHL playoff commitments.

While non–NHL playoff players were often parachuted in for tournaments like the world championships, a national team was formed for a season full of international events such as the Spengler Cup, Izvestia Cup and, up until 1994, the Olympics. NHL players were banned from the Olympics until 1988 and even then only a few NHL players would be released from NHL rosters for Olympic competition.

Version 2

The national team rose to prominence under the tutelage of head coach Dave King. For nine seasons, King pretty much was the Canadian national hockey program. Under his guidance, the national program gained immense credibility. King's ability to teach defence and the finer points of the game attracted junior stars such as Paul Kariya, Eric Lindros, Joe Juneau, Sean Burke, Patrick Flatley, Dave Gagner, James Patrick, Bob Joyce, Bruce Driver, Cliff Ronning, Trent Yawney, Zarley Zalapski, and Brian Bradley, to name but a few. The program became a welcome alternative to junior and minor league hockey and, in a few cases, even the NHL. Randy Gregg, Andy Moog, and Petr Nedved headline a long list of players who joined the program during their professional careers.

A former junior and collegiate coach, King found immediate success in international hockey when he coached Canada to the gold medal at the 1982 World Junior Championships and served as an assistant coach with the bronze medal–winning Team Canada at the 1982 World Championships.

He quickly took over the national team reins as head coach and in 1984 coached Canada to a fourth-place finish at the Olympic Games in Sarajevo. In 1986 he led Canada to the silver medal at the prestigious Izvestia tournament, and a year later the team captured the gold in the same Moscow tournament.

King returned to the Olympic Games in 1988 in Calgary, guiding Team Canada to a disappointing fourth-place finish on home ice. He would coach Canada in the world championships from 1989 to 1992, capturing silver medals in 1989 and 1991. He enjoyed his greatest Olympic success in the 1992 Games in Albertville, France, as he guided his team to the silver medal.

King would finally turn to the NHL following the '92 Olympics. Due to funding cuts and more and more professional intervention at international events, most notably full NHL participation in the Olympic Games starting in 1998, the national team program did not survive long after King's departure.

Here's a look at some of the players who brought us many memories during their seasons with the Canadian national team.

Three of the prime benefeciaries of Dave King's national team program combine to score on USA goalie Mike Richter. Bob Joyce (centre), Brian Bradley (left), and Serge Boisvert (right) all graduated to play in the NHL.

Glenn Anderson

Anderson was one of the first members of the reincarnated national team program. He is also arguably the most decorated graduate. The Vancouver native left the University of Denver to join the 1979–80 national team. His play there earned him a spot on the 1980 Olympic team where he chipped in with two goals and four points. He went on to the NHL where he quickly earned a reputation as a big game player. In addition to six Stanley Cup championships, Anderson was part of the 1984 and 1987 Canada Cup championship teams, as well as the silver medal winner in the 1989 world championships. Anderson always embraced the international game, and had two final stints with the Canadian national team as his career wound down. He played in a total of 119 games in a Team Canada uniform, scoring forty-five goals and eighty-eight points.

James Patrick

Known as an NHL veteran, Patrick got a taste of international hockey early in his career and made a habit of coming back to it whenever his NHL schedule would allow. Patrick was a star player with the standout University of North Dakota hockey program when he was summoned to Team Canada for the World Junior Championships in both 1982 and 1983. His experience there helped convince him to leave school early in order to play on the Canadian national team for the entire 1983–84 season, with hopes of making the Canadian Olympic team. It quickly became evident that Patrick was among the best players on the team, and he did participate in the Sarajevo Games. Patrick would turn pro immediately after the Olympics and quickly establish himself as a star with the New York Rangers. But he would return to Team Canada for five world championships plus the 1987 Canada Cup.

Brad Schlegel

The Kitchener, Ontario, native was an undersized but smooth-skating defenceman whose game was better suited to the international version than that of the NHL. Schlegel only played in forty-eight NHL games but had four full seasons with the Canadian

Schreiber would get into forty-one NHL games over the next two seasons, but when it became obvious he was destined for the minor leagues again, Schreiber embarked upon a lengthy professional career in Germany. But Schreiber always maintained a special place in his heart for Team Canada, and returned to represent Canada in both the 1992 and 1994 Olympic Games, earning a silver medal each time. He is one of only three male hockey players to represent Canada at the Olympics three times (Terry O'Malley and Eric Lindros are the others).

Vaughn Karpan

Vaughn Karpan never played a game in the NHL but he is a legendary hockey figure nonetheless. A University of Manitoba standout, Karpan rose to national prominence in four consecutive seasons with the Canadian national team. He joined the national program for the 1983–84 season and earned a spot on the Canadian Olympic team. He also earned a tryout with the Philadelphia Flyers of the NHL the following autumn, but when he was not offered a contract he returned to the national team for the next three seasons. In that time he established a record as the all-time games-played leader. He also won a silver medal at the Izvestia tournament in Moscow in 1986 and a gold medal at the same event in 1987. In 1988, Karpan participated in his second Olympic Games in Calgary. Karpan would retire shortly after those Games, but soon found NHL employment as a scout. He continues in that capacity with the Phoenix Coyotes.

Trent Yawney

Rather than develop in the minor leagues, Trent Yawney committed to Dave King's program for three seasons before maturing into an NHL defenceman. A solid prospect out of junior hockey, Yawney was drafted forty-fifth overall in the 1984 NHL entry draft by the Chicago Blackhawks. Unable to crack the Hawks lineup, the lanky Yawney developed his craft under King from 1985 to 1988, culminating with his captaining of the 1988 Olympic team for the Calgary Games. He would go on to a solid though quiet NHL career consisting of nearly 600 games. He would twice return to Team Canada at world championship time, playing with both the 1991 and 1992 squads.

Serge Boisvert

Despite his relatively small stature (five foot nine) Serge Boisvert scored at every level of hockey except the National Hockey League. During the 1988 Olympics in Calgary, Boisvert scored seven goals in eight contests. For that brief time he was the talk of hockey in Canada. Although such NHL veterans as Tim Watters, Steve Tambellini, Jim Peplinski, Andy Moog, and Randy Gregg bolstered this team, there was little Boisvert, leading the charge offensively.

Steve Tambellini

This speedy NHL veteran was one of three players released by NHL teams and parachuted onto Team Canada in an attempt to boost Canada's chances in the 1988 Olympics. He scored one goal and four points in those Calgary Games as his career wound down. Tambellini was no stranger to Team Canada and international hockey: his father, Addie, won a gold medal in the 1961 World Championships when amateur teams still represented the nation. In 1978 Tambellini played with

national team, plus parts of two others. In an era when Team Canada stocked its world championship roster with NHL talent who did not qualify for the Stanley Cup playoffs, Schlegel was still asked to represent his nation four times in that esteemed tournament. Schlegel's career highlight came in the 1992 Olympics when he captained Team Canada to a silver medal performance. He returned for the 1994 Olympics and captured a second silver medal.

Randy Gregg

Dr. Randy Gregg was one of the most vocal backers of the Canadian national team. Despite a career full of accomplishments with Team Canada and the dynastic Edmonton Oilers, you get the feeling that Gregg's biggest disappointment in his hockey life was never having a chance to play for Father Bauer's original national team in the 1960s. But Gregg helped to establish the values he shared with Bauer in two tours of duty with the Canadian national team. He participated with the Nationals for the 1979–80 season that climaxed with the Lake Placid Olympics. He would join the Oilers in 1982, and capture five Stanley Cups in the next ten years, but he interrupted his NHL career in 1987–88 in order to rejoin the national team and participate in his second Olympics, this time just down the road in Calgary. Gregg also accepted an invitation to represent Canada in the 1984 Canada Cup.

Wally Schreiber

After four seasons of tearing up the minor leagues with zero interest from the NHL, Schreiber joined the Canadian national team in 1986 and quickly earned some attention and eventually an NHL contract. He spent the 1986–87 and 1987–88 seasons with Team Canada as their offensive leader. He was then named to Canada's Olympic squad in the 1988 Calgary Games before getting his first shot at the NHL.

Wayne Gretzky in the World Junior Championships, and participated in the 1981 World Championships as well. Later, he would turn to a successful career as an administrator in both the NHL and international hockey. Tambellini served as a director of player personnel for both the 2001 World Championship team and 2002 gold medal–winning Olympic team. He returned as the general manager of the world championship team in 2002 and director of player personnel for the 2004 World Cup of Hockey.

Steve's son Jeff represented Team Canada at the 2004 World Junior Championships, making the Tambellinis the first three-generation family to represent Team Canada in international hockey.

Under the guidance of coach Dave King (opposite page), a host of players were given an extensive development program to hone their skills to NHL-calibre levels. Zarley Zalapski (above), guarding a Soviet opponent in a pre-Olympic game in 1988, and Brad Schlegel (right), guarding Trevor Kidd's doorstep in the early '90s, both earned opportunities to play NHL hockey.

The Canadian National Women's Hockey Team

DURING THE 1990S AND THROUGH THE TURN OF THE CENTURY, Canadians became excited by a group of new players representing Team Canada — female hockey players.

Women's hockey has existed in some shape or form in Canada since 1892, but it was not until the creation of the Women's World Hockey Championships in 1990 that the game was exposed to mass audiences. The women's game quickly rose in prominence, and by 1998 women were playing hockey in the Olympic Games.

Thanks to the exposure provided by the IIHF events and great television coverage, the women's game has blossomed around the globe. It is an exciting spectacle, with speed and skill on display. Violence is not tolerated in the women's game, but the only significant difference between men's and women's hockey is the banning of body checking in women's hockey.

Hockey Canada reports a 400 percent increase in female players in the last ten years, with 60,000 female players now registered. Meanwhile, the game has grown significantly internationally as well — twenty-six countries now participate in women's hockey.

At present Canada and the United States are the clear superpowers of the women's game. The two nations have had some epic clashes, particularly at the Olympics, and have a heated rivalry that draws fan attention almost as much as the men's rivalry. Canada has come out on top more often than not, capturing all eight of the World Championship titles to date. The United States gained some leverage by claiming the inaugural Olympic gold medal in 1998, but Canada redeemed itself on U.S. soil at the 2002 Salt Lake City Olympics to earn its first Olympic gold medal in women's hockey.

Here is a look at the players whose achievements have left an indelible mark on women's hockey and helped bring it to prominence.

Hayley Wickenheiser

Shaunovan, Saskatchewan's Hayley Wickenheiser is considered by most to be the best female hockey player of all time. She is a physically dominant player in the women's game, as she always grew up playing against boys. She has even played professional men's hockey in Europe and has twice gone to NHL rookie training camps with the Philadelphia Flyers.

A cousin of former NHLer Doug Wickenheiser, Hayley debuted with Team Canada as a fifteen-year-old on the team that won the 1994 World Championships. She went on to compete in the 1997, 1999, 2000, and 2004 World Championships, giving her a total of five gold medals. She would have won a sixth gold with the team in 2001 but missed the tournament with a knee injury.

Women's hockey hit the spotlight in 1998 when it became an Olympic sport. Wickenheiser, who was just nineteen years old, scored two goals and eight points in six games as Canada captured the silver medal. In 2002, Wickenheiser returned and powered Canada to a gold medal. Named to the Olympic All-Star team, she scored seven goals and ten points in five games to capture the gold from chief rivals Team USA.

Wickenheiser, who has also represented Canada at the Summer Olympics in fastball, is the closest thing to a household name in women's hockey. She has been recognized by *The Hockey News* as one of the one hundred most powerful people in all of hockey, and by the *Globe and Mail* as one of the most influential women in Canada today.

Jayna Hefford

Jayna Hefford scored the most famous goal in Canadian women's hockey history. In the gold medal game of the 2002 Olympics, Hefford scored on a beautiful breakaway with just one second remaining in the

Canada's domination of women's hockey has been broken only by the loss to the USA at the 1998 Olympic Games. Superstars like Hayley Wickenheiser (top) and Geraldine Heaney (right) have led Canada to victory in the 2002 Olympic Games as well as every women's world championship ever held. Above; the 1997 world champions celebrate in front of a jubilant crowd in Kitchener, Ontario.

second period in the famous game against the Americans. The goal proved to be the championship-winner. For Hefford it was sweet revenge, as she was also a part of the 1998 Olympic team that lost the first Olympic gold medal to Team USA.

Originally from Kingston, Ontario, Hefford has made a habit of scoring big and scoring often, particularly against the Americans. In fact she led the world in scoring in the 1999 and 2000 tournaments. In the 2000 World Championships, Hefford scored twice in the third period of the championship game to force overtime, which allowed Canada to salvage the gold. It is one of six world championship gold medals Hefford can hang around her neck.

Geraldine Heaney

A veteran of women's hockey, Geraldine Heaney is the only Canadian hockey player of either gender to capture seven world championships and an Olympic championship. She won the gold in seven women's world championships (1990, 1992, 1994, 1997, 1999, 2000, and 2001) and the Olympic gold in 2002. The star defender was also a member of the 1998 Olympic team that captured the silver medal.

Heaney has an interesting sidebar in her career biography. She was born in Northern Ireland, though raised in Canada. She had to acquire Canadian citizenship prior to the 1990 World Championships in order to play on Team Canada, making her the only female hockey player not born in Canada to play for the team. Several men have done this as well, including Stan Mikita, Peter Stastny, Petr Nedved, Dany Heatley, and Owen Nolan.

Cassie Campbell

The media love the charisma and poise of Cassie Campbell, and so too does the Canadian women's hockey team. Those two traits were significant reasons why she was named the Canadian captain for the 2002 Olympic Games. Campbell already had six world championships and an Olympic silver medal on her résumé, but captaining the 2002 gold medal Olympic team ranks as her greatest feat thus far.

The Brampton, Ontario, native is a superb skater and puckhandler, which has allowed her to become one of the most versatile assets on Team Canada. She has excelled both as a forward and a defenceman. Aside from Hayley Wickenheiser, Cassie Campbell ranks as the best-known Canadian women's hockey player. She may be more recognizable than Wickenheiser due to several television commercials and analyst appearances. She is also a popular guest at hockey schools across the country.

Danielle Goyette

The oldest player for Canada in the 2002 Olympics, Goyette was also the team's best player, tying Hayley Wickenheiser for the scoring lead with ten points in five games en route to capturing the gold medal. Goyette was also the leading Canadian goal scorer in the 1998 Olympics, where she earned a silver medal. Goyette participated in seven world championships, collecting another seven gold medals to make her one of the most decorated hockey players — male or female — in Canadian history. She leads all Canadian women in career goals at the national team level, scoring 92 times in 125 games.

Left, top: Top defender Therese Brisson launches an attack from the back against arch-rival USA.

Left, bottom: Cassie Campbell, versatile enough to play forward or defence, unleashes a slapshot from the point.

Below: Olympic heroine Jayna Hefford, whose dramatic second-period goal gave Canada the winning margin over the USA in the gold medal final at Salt Lake City.

The prolific left winger, born in St. Nazaire, Quebec, in 1966, was told by doctors prior to the 1998 Olympics that she should retire rather than risk more serious injuries. She has dislocated the same shoulder over twenty times, and has had several surgeries to try to repair the damage. But the veteran continues to play, and continues to be an offensive weapon for Team Canada. When she does retire, she will likely turn to coaching women's hockey, possibly at the international level.

Therese Brisson

Another veteran of Team Canada's women's hockey team, Brisson has six world championship gold medals, and Olympic gold and silver medals. A great blueliner, she captained Canada to the 1999, 2000, and 2001 World Championships.

Brisson, born in Dollard-des-Ormeaux, Quebec, began her journey of hockey excellence while studying at Concordia University in Montreal. She was so good at the collegiate level that she was inducted into the Concordia sports hall of fame. She valued her university days so much that she became a kinesiology professor at the University of New Brunswick, but training for Team Canada has forced her to put aside those career goals for the time being.

Vicky Sunohara

Scarborough, Ontario's Vicky Sunohara was a member of the original women's Team Canada back in 1990, but left the hockey scene soon after. She returned in 1996 and has been a regular ever since. She has six world championship gold medals, and Olympic gold and silver medals. While most members of the team remember the disappointment of finishing second to the United States, the silver medal may mean more to her than to any other member of the 1998 Olympic team: Sunohara's family originated in the Nagano, Japan, area and she became an instant celebrity in the host country.

Known as a power forward, faceoff specialist, and goal scorer, she has scored six game-winning goals at the world championships, a Canadian record. She is one of the top players in U.S. collegiate hockey history as well, leading Northeastern University to three consecutive Eastern College Athletic Conference (ECAC) titles.

France St. Louis

A physical education teacher from St. Hubert, Quebec, St. Louis is the grandmother of modern women's hockey and lacrosse. St. Louis was a prolific scorer in the days prior to the establishment of a Canadian national women's team, earning the Quebec "Female Athlete of the Decade" award for the 1980s. When the national and Olympic teams were formed, St. Louis was a natural selection, and the aging wonder became a defensive presence on the team. A faceoff specialist, St. Louis is a five-time world champion, twice while serving as team captain. St. Louis was a member of the 1998 Olympic team that won silver in Nagano, Japan. She retired in 1999 and now focuses on running hockey schools and promoting the great game of women's hockey.

World Cup 2004 and Beyond

Wayne Gretzky joins Team Canada's 2004 World Cup celebration, a victory that, along with the 2002 Olympic and 2004 World Championship titles, gives Canada unprecedented global hockey supremacy. Opposite page: Rising superstar Vincent Lecavalier earned MVP honors for the tournament.

PARITY HAS UNDOUBTEDLY ARRIVED IN INTERNATIONAL HOCKEY. Canada is one of seven nations that could win any international tournament. Russia, Slovakia, the United States, Sweden, the Czech Republic, and, most notably in 2004, Finland are equal threats to win any major tournament.

That being said, Canada has spent the early years of the new century sending a major message to the foreign competition: Canada intends to remain on top of the hockey world. Already holding back-to-back world championships and the Olympic gold medals in both the men's and women's events, Canada continued its quest for perfection with a 6-0 record in capturing the World Cup of Hockey 2004.

What is most notable about the 2004 victory is the transition of Canadian hockey from one generation to the next.

Just two years removed from the men's Olympic victory, Canada had many great young players emerge, forcing several prominent veterans aside. Gone were Paul Kariya, Eric Lindros, Al MacInnis, Brendan Shanahan, Mike Peca, Joe Nieuwendyk, and Owen Nolan. Injuries to Steve Yzerman, Rob Blake, Chris Pronger, and Ed Belfour forced Canada to go even younger. In just two short years, only ten Olympic gold medallists returned to represent Canada at the World Cup of Hockey.

As evidenced by the World Cup, this is definitely a positive transition. The next generation of Canadian talent is already pushing the bar and setting the stage for the next decade. There are many great moments to be had in the years to come, thanks to these future legends of Team Canada. Jarome Iginla, Vincent Lecavalier, Brad Richards, and Jay Bouwmeester headline Team Canada's next generation.

Iginla, a standout at the 1996 world juniors and 2002 Olympics, was back to cement his already impressive case for legendary status. He played exceptionally well on a line with Mario Lemieux and Joe Sakic, scoring two goals and three points in six games.

The Tampa Bay threesome of Stanley Cup champions Vincent Lecavalier, Brad Richards, and Martin St. Louis infused not only an immediate boost of skill and speed, but also a contagious and exuberant wave of youthful energy that inspired their fellow national team players. Lecavalier, a last-minute addition to replace Steve Yzerman, took his game to another level and earned the Most Valuable Player award. While upping his intensity and physical play to new heights, Lecavalier also displayed his wondrous creative instincts and puck-handling abilities, reminding many of a young Mario Lemieux.

Meanwhile, Brad Richards was reminiscent of a young Joe Sakic, thanks to his consistently elite level of clutch play. St. Louis added some scoring flair when needed, especially early in the tournament.

Richards and St. Louis found remarkable chemistry with Simon Gagne. Gagne, who debuted in 2002 on a line with Sakic and Iginla, is well on his way to legendary status. His consistent two-way play and his penalty-killing expertise have him looking like a Team Canada regular for the next number of years. The same can be said of Shane Doan, who was Canada's most aggressive forward and another great penalty killer. And Doan scored the decisive goal in the final game against Finland.

Joe Thornton and Dany Heatley look to be Canada's most exciting additions to top-level competition. Thornton in particular was impressive in the 2004 World Cup, joining the likes of Dale Hawerchuk, Lanny McDonald, and Steve Larmer in leaving his superstar status at home and gladly accepting a checking role. Thornton excelled, and was particularly dominant in the final game against Finland.

Teenage sensation Sidney Crosby will undoubtedly join them at some point as well. Other promising additions to come will be Patrick Marleau, Patrice Bergeron, Todd Bertuzzi, Alex Tanguay, Rick Nash, Jason Spezza, Eric Staal, Nathan Horton, Mike Richards, and Gilbert Brule.

Before the tournament began, Canada's group of blueliners at the 2004 World Cup of Hockey was a major point of concern. With MacInnis, Blake, and Pronger all gone with injuries, and with 2002 Olympian Ed Jovanovski falling to injury in the first period of the first game, much pressure was placed on Canada's only two veteran rear-guards—Adam Foote and Scott Niedermayer. The defence got even thinner when newcomer Wade Redden, the team's powerplay point-man, got hurt as well.

But Canada's four young defencemen excelled under pressure. Eric Brewer, just twenty-five, is already on track to become a legend of Team Canada with four world championships, including two gold medals, and the 2002 Olympic championship, under his belt. He came off a tough NHL season but re-established himself as an elite defender in the 2004 World Cup.

Three newcomers joined Brewer on the youthful blue line. Robyn Regehr, born in Racife, Brazil, pulled the Canadian jersey on for the third time in his career but for the first time at this level. He provided

the much needed physical presence that was missing with the absence of Pronger, Blake, and Jovanovski.

Then there was the young pairing of Scott Hannan and Jay Bouwmeester. They were only added to the team as injury replacements, and were slated strictly as number seven and eight defenders. But when forced into action, both played near-flawlessly. For Hannan, it was his first time wearing a Team Canada jersey, and he earned rave reviews.

Bouwmeester is the future of Canada's blue line. Though just twenty years old, Bouwmeester filled in and proved he belongs with the best in the world. His mobility and outlet passes added greatly to Canada's transition game. "J-Bo" is no stranger to international hockey, however, and he is well on his way to becoming a legend of Team Canada. He won back-to-back gold medals with Canada at the 2003 and 2004 World Championships. In 2003, he was chosen as the tournament's best defenceman. Bouwmeester also played for three Canadian world junior teams. In 2000, he was the youngest ever to play for Canada at a world junior at age sixteen years, three months.

Opposite page: Shane Doan swings around Finnish goalie Mikka Kiprusoff to score the winning goal in the 2004 World Cup.

Above: Goaltender Martin Brodeur celebrates victory with a Canadian flag adorning the goal crease.

2004 WORLD CUP OF HOCKEY STATS — *Team Canada*

Player	POS	GP	G	A	P	+/-	ESP	SHP	PPP	PIM
Vincent Lecavalier	C	6	2	5	7	1	5	0	2	8
Joe Sakic	C	6	4	2	6	4	5	0	1	2
Joe Thornton	C	6	1	5	6	4	5	0	1	0
Mario Lemieux	C	6	1	4	5	4	4	0	1	2
Kris Draper	C	5	2	2	4	5	4	0	0	2
Ryan Smyth	L	6	3	1	4	0	4	0	0	2
Eric Brewer	D	6	1	3	4	6	3	0	1	4
Martin St. Louis	R	6	2	2	4	1	2	0	2	0
Brad Richards	C	6	1	3	4	2	1	1	2	0
Adam Foote	D	6	0	3	3	7	3	0	0	0
Jarome Iginla	R	6	2	1	3	5	3	0	0	2
Scott Niedermayer	D	6	1	1	2	1	1	0	1	9
Shane Doan	R	6	1	1	2	4	2	0	0	2
Simon Gagne	L	6	1	1	2	2	1	1	0	0
Dany Heatley	R	6	0	2	2	0	2	0	0	2
Wade Redden	D	2	0	1	1	0	0	0	1	0
Scott Hannan	D	5	0	1	1	3	0	1	0	4
Ed Jovanovski	D	1	0	0	0	0	0	0	0	0
Brenden Morrow	L	1	0	0	0	0	0	0	0	4
Robyn Regehr	D	6	0	0	0	2	0	0	0	6
Jay Bouwmeester	D	4	0	0	0	3	0	0	0	0
Kirk Maltby	L	0	0	0	0	0	0	0	0	0
Patrick Marleau	C	0	0	0	0	0	0	0	0	0

Goaltender	GP	GA	SA	GAA	SV	SV%	SO	TOI	PIM
Martin Brodeur	5	5	129	1.00	124	.961	1	300	2
Roberto Luongo	1	3	40	2.82	37	.925	0	63:45	0
Jose Theodore	0	0	0	0	0	0	0	0	0

Key

POS – Position
GP – Games Played
G – Goals
A – Assists
P – Points

ESP – Even Strength Points
SHP – Short-Handed Points
PPP – Power-Play Points
PIM – Penalties in Minutes
+/- – Plus/Minus Average (the goal differential of a player on ice at even strength)

Goaltender Stats:
GP – Games Played
GA – Goals Against
SA – Saves
GAA – Goals Against Average

SV – Saves
SV% – Save Percentage
SO – Shutouts
TOI – Time On Ice
PIM – Penalties in Minutes

Canada will be looking for more new blood in the coming years. Brad Stuart, Derek Morris, Bryan McCabe, Kyle McLaren, Barret Jackman, Dion Phaneuf, and the always underrated Adrian Aucoin are all excellent candidates to carry on the Canadian tradition of physical, no-nonsense defence and puck-moving, mobile offence.

In goal, Martin Brodeur had his best international tourney yet, and he could play in a few more major tournaments, although he will have considerable pressure from the next generation of goaltenders.

Canada's depth in goaltending is the one area that appears to give Canada the greatest edge in the immediate future. Jose Theodore and Roberto Luongo backed Brodeur up at the 2004 World Cup of Hockey and are poised to take the torch should Brodeur ever relinquish it. Marc-Andre Fleury, Jean-Sebastien Giguere, and Marty Turco headline a seemingly endless supply of elite puck stoppers from Quebec. Every season seems to witness the arrival of another hot goalie. In the most important position of all, Canada looks strong and deep for years to come.

The 2004 World Cup victory confirmed Canada's place in the upper echelons of men's hockey. And with players like Sami-Jo Small, Cherie Piper, Tammy Lee Shewchuk, and Caroline Oullette, the women's side looks poised to lead Canada to further championships as well.

The future looks bright for Team Canada. There are some great international hockey events on the horizon and the nation will be well positioned to succeed in these tournaments. These players will carry the heavy burden of Team Canada's great history as they pursue hockey greatness. With a little luck, they'll win their share of championships. And one or two of the players may even join Paul Henderson, Phil Esposito, Wayne Gretzky, Mark Messier, Mario Lemieux, and the others as legends of Team Canada.

Hockey Canada's system for developing talent from an early age has allowed many top stars to represent their country at the Under-18 and World Junior championships. Graduates of this process who have reached the senior level team, or are likely to soon, include (clockwise from top left): Sydney Crosby, Anson Carter, Jay Bouwmeester, Dany Heatly, Joe Thornton, and Marc-Andre Fleury.

Bibliography

Bossy, Mike, with Barry Miesel. *Boss: The Mike Bossy Story.* McGraw-Hill Ryerson, 1988.

Diamond, Dan, (editor). *Total Hockey.* Total Sports Inc., 1998.

———— Second Edition. Total Sports Inc., 2000.

Dryden, Steve (editor). *The Hockey News Official Team Canada 2002 Magazine,* 2002.

Dryden, Steve (editor). *TSN Team Canada Collector's Edition,* The Sports Network 2002.

Gretzky, Wayne, with Rick Reilly. *Gretzky: An Autobiography.* Harper Collins, 1990.

McFarlane, Brian. *Team Canada 1972: Where Are They Now?* Winding Stair Press, 2001.

Podnieks, Andrew. *Canada's Olympic Hockey Teams: The Complete History, 1920-1998.* Doubleday Canada, Ltd., 1997.

Podnieks, Andrew. *Canadian Gold 2002.* Fenn Publishing Company, Ltd, 2002.

Podnieks, Andrew, et al. *Kings of the Ice: A History of World Hockey.* NDE Publishing, 2002.

Special thanks to:

Lucas Aykroyd

Ron Boileau

Arthur Chidlovski

Denis Gibbons

Kevin Gibson

Rebekah Hartberger

Patrick Houda

Michael Joyce

Jean-Patrice Martel

Stu McMurray

Joseph Nieforth

Charles Roth

Gene Suignard

Craig Wallace

Earl Zukerman

Photo Credits

Vantage Point Studios

Dan Hamilton - cover, 2, 6-7, 8(Gretzky), 9(Messier, world jr. team), 10, 36, 37, 38, 39, 40,41, 42, 43, 44, 45, 46, 47, 48, 49, 50, 51, 52, 53, 54, 55, 56, 57, 59, 60, 64, 68, 72, 73, 82-83, 84, 85, 86, 87, 88-89, 94-95(Carter, Heatley, Thornton, Fleury, Bouwmeester)

Ian Goodall - 9(women's team), 89(Hefford)

Bruce Jessop - 7(Ranford), 58, 61, 70, 71, 75

Roger Trudel - 77, 87(Brisson), 94(Crosby)

Denis Brodeur

8(Esposito, Orr), 9(bench), 11, 12, 13, 14, 15, 16, 17, 18, 19, 21, 22, 25, 26, 27, 28-29 30, 31, 32-33, 35

The Canadian Press

Uncredited - 78, 79

Blaise Edwards - 20, 23

Jeff Goode - 24

Larry MacDougall - 34

Tom Hanson - 62, 64

Jacques Boissinot - 63, 74

Rusty Kennedy - 66, 67

Frank Gunn - 69, 90, 91

Andre Forget - 75

Jeff Vinnick - 76

Adrian Wyld - 92, 93